GOOD WOOD

The Story of the Baseball Bat

Stuart Miller

ACTA SPORTS

GOOD WOOD
The Story of the Baseball Bat
by Stuart Miller

Edited by Gregory F. Augustine Pierce
Cover design by Tom A. Wright
Cover photo courtesy of Louisville Slugger Museum & Factory,
used with permission of Hillerich & Bradsby Co.
Text design and typesetting by Patricia A. Lynch

Published by ACTA Sports, a division of ACTA Publications, 4848 N. Clark Street, Chicago, IL 60077 (800) 397-2282 www.actapublications.com

Library of Congress Number: 2011939523
ISBN: 978-0-87946-477-6
Printed in the United States of America by McNaughton & Gunn
Year: 20 19 18 17 1615 14 13 12 11
Printing: 15 14 13 12 11 10 9 8 7 6 5 4 3 2 First

Contents

Introduction: BASEBALL'S ULTIMATE ICON 7

1: GETTING GOOD WOOD 13

2: SIZE DOES MATTER 21

3: THE REAL WONDERBOYS 35

4: SOME REAL CORKERS 57

5: A DANGEROUS WEAPON 71

6: EVOLUTION OF A WOODEN STICK 83

7: EXPLODING BATS 91

8: THE SLUGGER FROM LOUISVILLE 107

9: NOW BATTING 119

10: BATS BECOMING BATS 135

11: ADDING POP TO POP CULTURE 141

12: THE MVB AWARD 159

Epilogue: FUNGOES, BATBOYS, DOUGHNUTS, METAL BATS 169

Name Index 181

For the Superbas and Atlantics,
who give me an excuse to swing a bat every season.

BASEBALL'S ULTIMATE ICON

**There's nothing that feels as sweet
as a good, solid smash.**

Babe Ruth

The bat. Without one, baseball is reduced to a game of catch.

The baseball bat is an American icon, a symbol of power, inextricably linked with some of the greatest moments in sports history. It is often said, justifiably, that hitting a baseball is the most difficult feat in sports, so the bat—which can be whipped through the strike zone at speeds topping 115 miles per hour—is a most special tool. Among all the equipment used in baseball, football and basketball, only a fielder's glove rivals the bat in terms of individual affection and attention lavished on it, but rarely are the greatest Hall of Famers associated with their gloves.

A hitter often treats his weapon of choice in the same way royalty once treated the crown jewels, as something uniquely personal that requires the utmost care and protection. Yet bats are also subject to a player's whims and superstitions. Babe Ruth used to lay 20 bats on the ground and sample each one, looking for that certain, indefinable something, that perfect feel; Ted Williams rejected bats if they were a fraction of an ounce off (and he could tell); Yankees outfielder Roy White once changed bats every time up in a single game because none felt right, yet he ended up with five hits; in 1970 Mets outfielder Tommy Agee reportedly switched bats every game for 20 games as a slump-busting strategy (oddly, he hit safely in all 20 games but managed only 23 hits and a .288 average during that streak).

Enhancing the wooden bat's special stature is that it remains a work of beautiful simplicity. While technology continually revolutionizes our society, bats can be made from anything at hand. Generations of poor children, in the alleys behind New York tenements or in fields on Caribbean islands, have turned a broomstick into a faux Louisville Slugger. In Germany during World War II, some American soldiers spent their spare time carving bats from trees so they could play ball. One of the game's most beloved images is a photo of Willie Mays at a makeshift plate on the streets of Harlem, wielding nothing more than a stickball bat. Out for a winter's walk on the frozen Hudson River last year, my two sons picked up a branch, packed some snow into a ball and began playing baseball.

When a hitter breaks a bat on a base hit, the saying goes that the bat "dies a hero." Here's another thought you might want to bat around: Bats are such an intrinsic part of American culture that they pop up (not in the just-missed-a-high-heater kind of way) repeatedly in American phraseology. You'll "go to bat for" a friend, especially someone you liked "right off the bat."

When I was seven years old, my uncle took me to Game 4 of the 1973 National League Championship Series between my beloved New York Mets and Cincinnati's Big Red Machine. In the seventh inning, with the Mets leading 1-0 and mere outs from clinching a World Series berth, my uncle's colleague told me that Tony Perez could tie the game "with one swing of the bat," which Perez promptly did. In the 12th inning, this same guy told me that Pete Rose could untie the game "with one swing of the bat," which Rose promptly did. Not surprisingly, I was distraught. And while the Mets prevailed in the National League Championship Series, I've played that phrase in my head ever since, likening the power of a bat to a modern-day Excalibur.

Bats do create kings, of a sort, and the numerous nicknames bats have inspired throughout the years certainly draw a link to knights going off to battle. They've been called a shillelagh, a mace, a bludgeon, a willow, a cudgel, a war club, and even "the Death Stick" (by a 13-year-old whom I coach in Brooklyn). Ty Cobb referred to the bat as a "wondrous weapon" and probably meant it literally. Big George Scott used the more prosaic appellation "lumber," but with menacing overtones—"If you want to rumble, just touch my lumber."

In the 1970s, outfielder Jay Johnstone had a nickname more appropriate for the free-agent era, calling his bat "my business partner," while Orioles speedster Al Bumbry chose a more poetic approach and one that acknowledged the bat as a Freudian phallic symbol: He referred to his bat as "my soul pole."

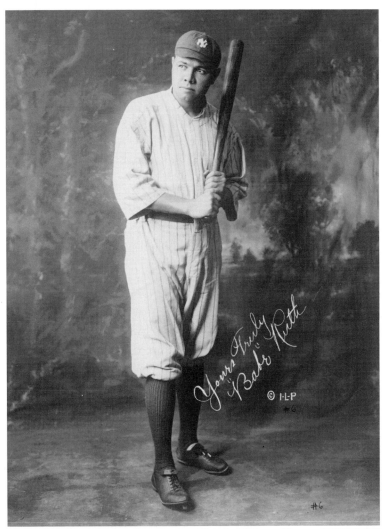

Photo Credit: Library of Congress, LC-USZC4-7246

Babe Ruth shown with a bat in 1920, his first year with the Yankees, when the Bambino hit 54 home runs and had a .376 batting average.

Each player has a different relationship with the stick he swings. Bo Jackson, who was known for so many astonishing feats on the baseball and football fields, created one of his most memorable when he broke a bat over his head after striking out. (Jackson also broke bats across his leg, but other players have done that since, often hotheads like Milton Bradley or Carlos Zambrano.) Long ago, when bat handles were nearly as thick as the barrel, Cleveland Indians star Joe Sewell reportedly used one bat for 14 years. In more recent times, sluggers have gone for lighter bats by choosing thinner handles, leading to far more broken bats—Pete Incaviglia supposedly broke over 100 in one season (estimates have ranged from 114 to 144). Outfielder Curtis Granderson attracted attention while with the Detroit Tigers in 2006 for using a maple bat that looked as if it had been around since Sewell's time. In fact this particular black bat lasted only a couple of weeks, but it showed off every scuff mark from foul balls—and other wear and tear as well. While in the on-deck circle, Granderson used a long donut and applied it upside down. ("It just feels better," he explained.) The donut causes the paint to chip, and Granderson further dirtied his bat with an extra-sticky pine-tar alternative. The overall result was a tattered-looking bat—one that drew plenty of comments. Granderson didn't mind. "There was an added bonus," he said. "Pitchers could see that no one had gotten inside on me, and that intimidates them a little bit."

Major league players aren't the only ones who love their bats—Louisville Slugger has made bats for U.S. presidents, a pope, and Elvis Presley. Each year, nearly a quarter of a million visitors trek to the Louisville Slugger Factory and Museum in Kentucky. (And while there aren't as many sandlot games as

Photo Credit: National Baseball Hall of Fame

American soldiers during World War II turned to baseball to ease homesickness, going so far as to carve bats out of tree limbs so they could play a game.

Photo Credit: Sharon Seitz.

Prospect Park (Brooklyn) Baseball Association wooden bats lined up in a dugout in 2011.

there once were, where kids go hand-over-hand on a baseball bat to see who bats first, bats remain a necessity for that other childhood staple: the dizzy bat race.)

We all can conjure up the image of the classic bat. Perhaps it is being wielded at the plate by our favorite player, or swung in our memories by a Little League version of ourselves. It might be as a symbol of potency, as in the vintage portraits of Brooklyn's Boys of Summer with Jackie Robinson, Duke Snider, Gil Hodges, and Roy Campanella all pointing their bats together, or perhaps instead it is a poignant symbol, as in the photo of an ailing Babe Ruth leaning on his bat like it was a cane in his final visit to Yankee Stadium. But bats, while they remain the same in essence, have evolved and continue to do so, from heavy to light, from thick to skinny handles, from hickory to ash to maple (with a side helping of aluminum, bamboo, and other ingredients thrown in at the amateur level).

This book will take you on a journey through the rich and storied—and occasionally nefarious—story of the baseball bat and those who have made them and swung them. This version of the story is more eclectic than comprehensive: I haven't covered every small bat company, or every player's quirk, or all the famous hits, or every instance of cheating with a bat. But by book's end, I think you will be inspired to dig out your favorite wooden stick and take a few hacks in the backyard or at your local batting cage.

So grab a bat and step up to the plate.

Stuart Miller
Brooklyn, New York
Fall 2011

Chapter 1

GETTING GOOD WOOD
Looking for—and creating—the perfect bat

> The pitcher has got only a ball. I've got a bat.
> So the percentage in weapons is in my favor
> and I let the fellow with the ball do the fretting.

Hank Aaron

When Ted Williams showed up for his first spring training, the young lefthanded hitter toted with him a cheap store-bought bat that had the veterans chuckling.

Soon enough, however, Williams established himself not only as one of baseball's greatest hitters but also as the game's most sophisticated and rigorous bat connoisseur. Williams ordered 35-inch bats, preferring a medium barrel and a narrow grain. He liked a light bat, so he mostly swung 33-ouncers during his career, although he'd go as low as 32 late in a season. He'd developed the habit of lowering the bat weight in his last minor league season. One night when he'd started feeling worn down, the young hitter picked up a teammate's light bat and proceeded to hit a 410-foot grand slam. Williams was converted to the notion that lighter bats can produce plenty of power because a hitter can generate more bat speed.

Williams was so committed to getting the perfect Louisville Slugger that he began traveling each spring to Kentucky, where he would climb up onto batmaker Hillerich & Bradsby's pile of raw timber to select his own wood. He insisted on having 10 grains or fewer per inch (some players, like Willie Mays, have preferred wider grains), used a special mix of olive oil and resin for his bat's grip, and refused to let his bats be transported in the cargo sections of airplanes or lie on the grass during games—all to protect his precious bats from the humidity. Williams also made certain Boston's equipment manager took his bats into the clubhouse immediately after games—not just ahead of other bats but even before anyone on the team left the field. Then he'd clean them with alcohol every night. He also got the Red Sox to put a scale in the clubhouse so he could constantly check to see if his bats had gained weight from dirt or moisture.

Photo Credit: National Baseball Hall of Fame

Ted Williams made a science of hitting, so naturally the wood implements used by the Splendid Splinter received his close personal attention.

All this was a far cry from the early days of baseball, when players would often just grab any bat that was handy, whether it belonged to a teammate or even an opponent.

One time Williams returned a shipment of bats to the Louisville Slugger company, complaining that the handle width was off. Bat-factory employees measured the width with calipers and found the discrepancy to be $5/1,000^{th}$ of an inch. Another time, Williams barked about the varying weight of the bats. So, according to Williams' book *The Science of Hitting*, Louisville Slugger company president John Hillerich took six unmarked bats—with five weighing exactly the same and one a half-ounce off—and asked Williams to close his eyes and pick out the heavier bat.

According to Williams, he got it right twice in a row. (There may be a bit of legend mixed in to this story, which changes with different tellings. In one variation, Hillerich had bats each weighing a half-ounce more than the last, mixed them up, and then asked Williams to put them in order by weight. In this version, Williams got the test right five times in a row.)

In 1957 the Splendid Splinter hit an amazing .388 at the superannuated age of 39. Citing this performance as his greatest accomplishment, he gave some of the credit to changing bats. At the start of the year, he switched to a 34½-ounce bat that was about two ounces heavier than what he'd been using. He said this not only enabled him to hit the ball harder but also slowed his swing just enough to make him hit the ball the other way more often. That foiled the "Williams Shift"—first used by Indians manager Lou Boudreau a decade earlier and now a staple of Major League Baseball—in which three infielders played on the right side of the diamond. Having forced American League defenses to rethink

their alignment, Williams then switched back to the lighter bat at midseason of '57, enabling him to stay fresh and also to resume pulling the ball to the right side, where openings had reappeared with the shift gone.

Ted Williams isn't the only hitter to pay close attention to his lumber. In today's game, the most particular players seem to be, like their bats, Japanese imports. Just as Williams worried about humidity, Seattle's human hitting machine, Ichiro Suzuki, stores his bats in a sealed alumi-

Photo Credit: Mizuno

Mizuno's legendary Isokazu Kubota has been meticulously crafting bats for players like Hideki Matsui for over half a century.

num case in the dugout to protect them from moisture and also uses a humidor for them. And Kosuke Fukudome nearly matches Williams' fanaticism about bat weight; while he uses a 35-inch, 35-ounce bat during spring training to build up strength, during the season he is known for keeping a portable scale handy to make sure every bat weighs exactly 920 grams or 32.4 ounces. Then there's Hideki Matsui. When he left the comfort of success in Japanese baseball to try to make it in the United States, he knew he had one extremely important weapon in his arsenal—a bat made by Mizuno's master craftsman, Isokazu Kubota.

Matsui, whose first pro bat was made of Japanese ash but resembled the bamboo wood composite he had used in high school, began having bats made by Kubota when he broke in with the Yomiuri Giants in 1993. From the beginning, the two men clicked, each heeding the other's suggestions. Matsui listened to the veteran bat-maker's advice that he not change bats each time he hit a rough stretch—such fickleness made it impossible to determine what the problem really was—and Kubota carefully fine-tuned Godzilla's bats each season, per the player's requests.

Matsui wanted his 35-inch, 31½-32-ounce bat to be similar to that of Japan's three-time Triple Crown winner, Hiromitsu Ochiai, so each season Kubota brought him a little closer to that objective, giving him a bat with a slightly smaller sweet spot and a thinner-but-heavier barrel that packed more punch. Matsui's home run totals jumped from the low 20s to the upper 30s and then the 40s before topping out at 50 in his final season in Japan.

But when Matsui joined the New York Yankees in 2003, he reversed course. Having shrunk his sweet spot from 1.98 inches to 1.76, he asked Kubota to expand it to 1.90 for his new "rookie" season. "Major league pitchers can be more deceptive," Kubota explained at the time. Matsui's take: "Major leaguers throw a lot of moving fastballs, so I have to make the sweet spot wider or I won't be able to make contact."

The adjustment worked. In his first three seasons in the U.S., Matsui's home run totals plunged—he averaged 23 a year—but he built a reputation as a professional hitter by batting .297 and averaging over 40 doubles and 110 RBI.

Edgar Martinez was very particular about his bats too. Martinez defined the designated hitter position after settling into the role in 1995, hitting an American League-leading .356 in his first DH season and following up with averages of .327, .330, .322, .337, and .324. Martinez's bat was of relatively normal proportions, but he had a quirk—the Seattle Mariners star liked bats made at various weights. Against a certain pitcher or in a particular situation, he didn't want a 31-ounce bat (too light) or one weighing 31.5 ounces (too heavy); instead, his bat had to be custom-made at a just-right-for-him 31.2 ounces. (Many switch hitters use different weights from each side of the plate—Atlanta's Chipper Jones swings a 34-ounce natural-finish bat from the left side and a 33-ounce black bat from the right side.)

Some players worry less about fractions of ounces and more about whether the bat's sweet spot makes sweet music. Nineteenth-century star Hugh Duffy bounced billets (raw wood sticks) off a concrete floor—before the wood was shaped into a bat—and listened for a ring. It is a trend that has bounced back, so to speak, in recent years. In the 1990s, big hitters like Edgar Martinez, Dante Bichette, Vinny Castilla, and Cecil Fielder were all "ping practitioners," holding a new bat up to their ear, tapping the end, and listening for the bat's pitch. A high tone supposedly equaled solid wood and thus became a game bat, a low or dead tone was consigned to batting practice or the scrap heap. As a young player, Carlos Beltran picked the habit up from Martinez while standing around the batting cage before a Seattle-Kansas City game and has helped bring this tradition into the twenty-first century

Other players view bats more like a Lay's Potato Chip—they can't

Photo Credit: Library of Congress, LC-USZC4-6864

In the last two decades, players such as Edgar Martinez and Carlos Beltran have picked up the habit of bouncing their bats, deciding the quality of each bat based on its pitch. But a century ago, Hugh Duffy used to bounce an entire billet on the floor to see if its sound made the wood even worthy of being carved into a bat.

stop with just one. Johnny Mize, who led the National League in homers four times from 1939 through 1948, took the multiple choice concept to extremes. The Big Cat was a man of many bats. He reportedly had 60 varieties of bats, making his selection depending on the situation or the pitcher. Against fellow southpaws, for example, he relied on longer bats to attack pitches that tailed away.

Negro Leagues star Turkey Stearnes lacked Mize's heft but matched him in terms of clout. A left-handed-hitting slugger who also hit for a good average, Stearnes had several idiosyncrasies. For example, he earned his nickname by flapping his arms while running the bases. At the plate, Turkey dug his front foot into the ground and pointed his toes at the sky. With bats, he was like Mize, owning different bats for specific situations, although his selections seemed less scientific and more superstitious than Mize's. He supposedly had a bat for hitting the ball off the outfield wall and another for hitting homers. Also, Stearns gave his bat verbal instructions before each plate appearance.

Many players think that superstars get special treatment from the bat manufacturers. In the 1950s Yankees infielders Gil McDougald and Andy Carey ordered some of Yogi Berra's bats from Louisville Slugger, figuring that the future Hall of Famer was getting better quality wood than they were. In the 1980s Braves third baseman Ken Oberkfell ordered Dale Murphy's bats, and in the 1990s some Reds players were known to ask for Barry Larkin's bats.

On the other hand, being a great hitter sometimes means your bats are the most vulnerable to theft. Former Yankee Don Mattingly says that when he was on the road, someone invariably would steal one of his bats from the clubhouse in every city. "They would look on the handle, and see my number, 23, written there, and grab one," he says. Mattingly mostly used Louisville Slugger model T141 in his prime, preferring an unfinished look; his bats were 34 inches and usually 31 or 32 ounces. He sometimes outsmarted the thieves by using the numbers 5 or 7 on his bats, knowing that not only would this deter prospective thieves from identifying his bats easily but he also didn't have to worry that a teammate might mistake a Mattingly bat for his own because the numbers 5 (Joe DiMaggio) and 7 (Mickey Mantle) had long been retired by the Yankees.

And while star players often do get the choice lumber from the big bat-makers, just being one of the best hitters in baseball isn't enough—staying true to your bat-maker apparently counts too. "We have a priority list of players," says Chuck Schupp, head of the pro bat division at Louisville Slugger. "If someone is loyal to us, we'll take care of them. If I turn on the TV and see a guy who has

Photo Credit: National Baseball Hall of Fame

Johnny Mize reportedly had about 60 bats at any one time and would choose different ones for different situations or pitchers.

signed with us using three different [manufacturers'] bats in a game, he's not going to get the priority of someone who uses our bat 100 percent of the time."

To ensure obtaining the best wood of all, some players like Alex Rodriguez have followed Williams' footsteps to the Louisville Slugger factory. In the end, determining what makes the best possible bat is the subject of ongoing debate. Many players see pin knots as a defect in a bat, but others—Babe Ruth and Carl Yastrzemski included—liked them, thinking the characteristic indicated a tougher wood.

The major argument about what constitutes "good wood" is about grains. Many players prefer wide grains, which indicate a faster-growing tree, a hot summer and a warm winter, but others, including the meticulous Williams, argued that tighter grains make tougher bats. Scientific studies support the latter group, indicating that narrow-grain bats, which come from slower-growing trees, are the strongest and most durable. Louisville Slugger veteran bat-maker Danny Luckett, who favors the narrow-grained bat, knows even scientific data won't end these debates. "Players are the most superstitious bunch of people you will ever meet," he says. "They're all nuts."

Chapter 2

SIZE DOES MATTER
Stories of Weird Bats and Batters

> I never blame myself when I'm not hitting.
> I just blame the bat, and if it keeps up, I change bats.
> After all, if I know it isn't my fault that I'm not hitting,
> how can I get mad at myself?

Yogi Berra

Ladies and Gentlemen, size does matter…at least when it comes to baseball bats.

Some players have swung long, heavy bats and others have preferred short, light lumber. Heavy bats were most common in the dead-ball era, when players wanted to get good wood on the ball and place it just so for a single. Few exemplified this better than Edd Roush, who swung what tied for the heaviest bat in modern major league history—a thick-handled stick weighing a whopping 48 ounces. Babe Ruth ordered bats topping 50 ounces but usually used them only in spring training and rarely went above 47 ounces in a game.

Roush grew up on a farm and developed immensely strong wrists and hands while milking cows. The lefty Roush was a fiery competitor and incredibly fast, too, perhaps second only to Tris Speaker as a defensive outfielder in his time. But the Cincinnati Reds star was best known for the way he wielded his heavy artillery: Roush had a lifetime average of .323 over 18 years; he won National League batting titles in 1917 and 1919 and finished second by just percentage points in 1918; he also averaged .350 from 1921-24. The Hall of Famer accomplished all this with his devotion to place-hitting line drives, a technique he called "glorified bunting." His bat's heft was essential to his success: "I only take a half swing at the ball, and the weight of the bat rather than my swing is what drives it." (A catcher named Hank Severeid from the same era also used a 48-ouncer but is largely forgotten, in part because Roush tallied over three thousand more plate appearances and had two batting titles to his credit.)

Roush and Severeid had two rivals for heaviest bludgeon. Mule Suttles reportedly used a 50-ounce bat to hammer balls into the bleachers, but Suttles was black during the age of segregation, so his stardom was unfortunately limited to the Negro Leagues. Hack Miller, who had two glorious seasons with the Chicago Cubs in the 1920s, used a 47-ounce bat but occasionally would haul a bat he said was 65 ounces to the plate, in part, he said, because he'd never feel any sting using such a heavy stick. Miller was the son of a circus strongman and was largely considered the strongest man in baseball—he could supposedly hold a bat above his head with a teammate dangling off from each side. But he was also muscle-bound, overweight, and slow, and spent most of his careering pounding homers in the minor leagues (where, he claimed, he sometimes swung a 67-ounce club).

Roush's bat was heavy, but not overly long—much of the weight was in the thick handle. The longest stick in modern baseball belonged to Philadelphia A's star Al Simmons, who swung a 38-inch bat. The right-handed-hitting Simmons was a fearsome offensive player with a fierce approach. "He'd squeeze the handle of that doggone thing and throw the barrel of that bat toward the pitcher in his warmup swings," longtime Yankee Tommy Henrich once said, "and he would look so bloomin' mad—in batting practice…. He was one angry man at home plate."

Simmons, who said he hated pitchers, had a most unusual stance, pointing his left (front) foot toward the third base line and deliberately pulling off the ball as he swung. This approach of "stepping in the bucket" is usually criticized because it deprives a hitter of plate coverage and power. But thanks to his vicious swing and extra-long bat, Bucketfoot Al (a nickname he deplored) managed to get to just about any pitch and drive it—as his dazzling statistics proved. He was a terror from 1925-31, hitting above .380 four times in that span and winning two American League batting crowns. He had at least 100 RBI in each of his first 11 major league seasons and hit 307 career home runs.

At the other end of the spectrum was Willie Keeler. When your nickname is Wee Willie, it makes sense you would use a short stick. The 5'4½", 140-pound Keeler did just that, making baseball history by using a 30-incher (the same length used by 11 and 12 year old Little Leaguers today). The Brooklyn-born star came up with the New York Giants in 1892. Scorned by the Giants as too small, he moved on to National League rivals Brooklyn and Baltimore and became a star with the Orioles in 1894, when he began a run of eight consecutive years with at least 200 hits. In 1897 Keeler batted .424 and established the National League record with a 44-game hitting streak. (Pete Rose tied the mark in 1978.) Here's the catch, so to speak: Keeler's bat was small, but it was no lightweight. In keeping with the dead-ball times, Keeler "hit 'em where they ain't" with a heavy piece of lumber—his 30-inch bats often weighed 46 ounces, nearly as heavy as Edd Roush's record-setter.

Photo Credit: National Baseball Hall of Fame

Wee Willie Keeler's bat, placed below a typical bat of the time, was just 30 inches long, but during his career he found plenty of room on the barrel to use it to place the ball where there were no fielders.

Meanwhile, baseball lore credits Billy Goodman and Joe Morgan with wielding the lightest bats in major league history. Both used 30-ouncers. Goodman, a big-league infielder from 1947-1962, was essentially the same size as Edd Roush (5'11", 165-170 pounds) and also a slap hitter. Playing for the Red Sox in 1950, Goodman led the American League in hitting at .354; plus, he batted above .300 four other times. Morgan, the Hall of Famer and two-time National League MVP, tipped the scales at just 155 pounds, yet he slammed 268 career homers, topping 20 in a year four times.

Yet neither is the true record-holder for lightest lumber used. That honor belongs to Solly Hemus, the starting shortstop for the Cardinals from 1951-53 and an 11-year major leaguer. Hemus said he used a heavy bat in the minors and used it to punch the ball, but when he arrived in St. Louis he listened to Stan Musial about the importance of a light bat in generating bat speed to gain power.

Photo Credit: National Baseball Hall of Fame

Stan "The Man" Musial ordered bats with skinny handles—just 15/16 of an inch thick—but then shaved the handles down more with bottle caps.

"He was using a 31-ounce bat and he's a lot bigger than me," the 5'9", 165-pound Hemus said of Musial, a 6-footer who played at 180 pounds.

So after hitting just two homers in his rookie year, Hemus, who mostly used Adirondacks, switched to a 34-inch, 29-ounce bat, which he made even lighter by shaving the handle down (a la Musial) to improve his wrist action. Sure, he said, some guys teased him about the toothpick he was swinging, but Hemus never let it bother him, especially when he banged out 29 four-baggers over the next two seasons. "With the lighter bat, I had more confidence and could pull the ball," he said.

Any talk of small and light bats ultimately ends with Eddie Gaedel. His bat was the tiniest ever used in a major league game, although "used" is a stretch, because the 17-inch, 23-ounce bat never left his shoulder. The appearance of Gaedel, a midget, in a 1951 game was the brainchild of Bill Veeck, baseball's greatest maverick and promotional genius. Then owner of the lowly St. Louis Browns, Veeck concocted perhaps his most famous publicity stunt when he had a seven-foot cake taken to the field between games of a doubleheader against Detroit—ostensibly to celebrate the 50th anniversary of the American League—and arranged for the 3'7", 65-pound Gaedel to pop out. Gaedel was wearing a Browns uniform with the number ⅛ (and elf-like slippers). The fun, as it turned out, was only beginning.

In the first inning, Gaedel was sent up as a pinch hitter for Browns right fielder Frank Saucier. Veeck had impressed upon Gaedel the importance of using an exaggerated crouching stance to enhance the effect of his small size; he also ordered the first-time-ever hitter not to swing the bat under any circumstances during the at-bat.

Gaedel's miniscule strike zone, of course, prompted a protest from the Tigers, but the Browns produced a signed contract. Tigers pitcher Bob Cain then tried in vain to get the ball over the plate but walked Gaedel on four pitches. Gaedel, who had been paid $100, went to first base, took his hat off and bowed to the crowd before being removed for a pinch runner. He received a standing ovation.

"Man, I felt like Babe Ruth," said Gaedel, who was released the next day when American League president Will Harridge refused to approve his contract.

Eddie Gaedel's bat was merely a novelty. Heinie Groh's bat also looked like a stunt, but his "bottle bat"—with a bulging barrel that dropped off with a "bottleneck" instead of gradually tapering down to the handle—was, in fact, a formidable weapon.

Groh struggled in the minors, hitting .161 in his first season, but he made it to the New York Giants in 1912. Manager John McGraw, perhaps baseball's most knowledgeable and opinionated man (take Bobby Valentine and multiply him by five), told Groh he didn't like the bat that the rookie was using. Get one with a larger barrel, the legendary manager decreed. But in those dead-ball days, big-barreled bats meant thick handles. There was no way that Groh, a 5'7", 160-pound infielder with small hands, could get a good grip.

Groh went to the Spalding company in New York and, as he explained in Lawrence Ritter's *The Glory of Their Times*, "We went down in the basement and right there we whittled on a bat until it was just what I needed."

After slimming down the standard bat handles, Groh had the Spalding bat-makers bulk up the barrels so the bats resembled "a crazy sort of milk bottle," featuring the big bulge and the sharp drop to the skinny handle. The bats weighed around 45 ounces. Although they were short, he had requested an extra-long handle because he choked up and kept his hands a little apart.

Even if a hitter wanted to hold a bottle bat at the knob end, he couldn't because the weight distribution would result in the bat getting knocked out of his hands every time. Because Groh choked up so much, however, he had that big barrel near his hands so he could fist an inside pitch over the infield without breaking the bat.

McGraw soon traded the youngster, only to regret it. Using this unique model bat, Groh managed only 26 homers in 6,074 at-bats over 16 seasons, but he was able to bunt, punch, and slap hits to the tune of a .292 career average. Playing for Cincinnati, Groh led the National League in hits in 1917 and twice paced the league in doubles. Reacquired by McGraw after the 1921 season, Groh batted .474 for the Giants in the 1922 World Series. (According to Dan Gutman's book *Banana Bats and Ding-Dong Balls*, one of Groh's original bats was used as a prop during the making of *Zelig*, Woody Allen's film about a man who shows up in every imaginable historic circumstance, but the bat was accidentally broken during filming.)

Groh's reshaping of his bats was an extreme example, but plenty of other major leaguers have made smaller—sometimes even minute— adjustments in their bats, with results that speak for themselves.

Hack Wilson was a muscular 190-pounder with a thick neck, broad shoulders, and an imposing chest. But he stood only 5'6", wore size-6 shoes, and had correspondingly small hands (with stubby fingers to boot). Accordingly, he always requested bats with exceedingly thin handles. Unlike Groh, he did not want a bat tailored to punch at the ball. The long ball was Wilson's specialty—the Cubs' slugger came of age in the high-flying 1920s, leading the National League in homers three consecutive years. In 1930, he crushed 56 homers—the National League record for nearly seven decades—and drove in 191 runs, a still-standing major league mark. Those thin handles obviously worked for him.

Jeff Bagwell, the 1991 N.L. Rookie of the Year and 1994 MVP, came of age when everyone wanted an ultra-slim handle, one that replicated the feel of the aluminum bats used at the amateur level. But with wood, these bats became too top-heavy for Bagwell, so the Astros' standout had Louisville Slugger create a large flare on the knob to improve the balance.

But even after a bat is crafted to meet a player's every desire, some feel compelled to keep going, making further adjustments. In the modern era, few hitters could match the skill of Stan Musial, who earned three MVP awards on the way to a .331 career batting average and 475 homers. And no one used a skinnier handle than the Cardinals' legend. Stan the Man ordered bats with handles that were only $^{15}/_{16}$ of an inch thick—but even that wasn't thin enough for him. He would shave down the handle even more with bottle caps. Longtime Houston Astro Craig Biggio brought his own approach to Musial's technique, sanding down his handle with his own equipment, then taping it back up a little. Outfielder Scott Podsednik, of 2005 White Sox World Series fame, disliked feeling a knob at the end of his bat, so he cut off the knob off and stuck one layer of tape at the bottom

Many personalized bat adjustments are less immediately noticeable. Historically, the most common approach to bat preparation involved strengthening the wood by "boning" or "bone-rubbing" it. Players rubbed a hard object endlessly over their bats—animal bones were most common. Some teams, like the Phillies of the 1940s, kept a mounted hambone attached to a table in the clubhouse. Longtime Chicago Cubs first baseman Mark Grace favored the cow femur. But baseball players are an inventive bunch and have used glass cola bottles, rolling pins, and even other bats to hone their bats. In his Hall of Fame career, catcher Gary Carter, of the Montreal Expos and New York Mets, preferred a porcelain sink.

"Boning helps close the pores and harden the bat's surface, making it more durable and providing more power," says Chuck Schupp, Louisville Slugger's point person for pro players.

Yet boning is becoming a lost art. In part, it's because some scientists have questioned the value. Another factor, Schupp explains, is that today's young players "open the box and expect their bat to just be ready. They say, 'What do you mean I have to do something to it? I just want to hit with it.'"

But bat-making trends are the biggest reason for the drop-off in boning. Maple bats already have a compressed grain and don't flake and chip the way ash does, so boning them is unnecessary; also, any bat with a lacquer finish can't be bone-rubbed because it would destroy the finish.

Given how obsessed players can be with their bats, it's hardly surprising that ballplayers over the years have tried countless alternatives to boning, al-

Photo Credit: Library of Congress, LC-USZ62-78818

Honus Wagner, the Flying Dutchman, took great care with his bats, boiling them in creosote as a preservative.

ways looking to strengthen and preserve their bats. The Pirates' Honus Wagner, among the greatest hitters of the early 20th century, reportedly boiled his bats in creosote, an oily and often-yellowish liquid that comes from the distillation of wood tar or coal tar. The liquid was commonly used as a wood preservative, although it was extremely toxic and could cause neurological problems if inhaled to a significant degree.

According to baseball lore, Hall of Fame second baseman star Eddie Collins toughened up his bats by burying them in a dunghill. Frankie Frisch, of Giants and Cardinals fame, supposedly hung his bats in a barn to "cure" them, as if they were dried meat—a technique reminiscent of 19th-century standout Cap Anson, who hung his collection of 500 bats in his cellar. (Anson also bought fence posts and logs and had them made into bats.) Jim Frey, who reached the majors only as a manager but won two minor league batting championships, soaked his bats in motor oil. Atlanta Braves slugger Dale Murphy rubbed alcohol on his bats, and the New York Mets' Howard Johnson put dirt on his, covered them with sticky pine tar and then repeatedly slammed a weighted batting doughnut over the bats until the dirt and pine tar filled in the grain.

Not every player thought "treating" a bat meant boning or curing or rubbing oil on it. Some simply pampered their favorites. When Richie Ashburn, who won two batting titles for the Phillies in the 1950s, was on a hot streak, the fleet center fielder was known to sleep with his stick. "When you're going good, you want to take care of your bat," Ashburn explained. In the 1970s, Jose Morales nurtured his bat by taking it wherever he went and occasionally smothering it with kisses; in the '80s, Leon Durham had his mother pray over his bats.

Before Shoeless Joe Jackson earned lasting infamy as the biggest star

Photo Credit: National Baseball Hall of Fame

Shoeless Joe Jackson gave his bats special treatment with a sweet oil, took them south for the winter, and gave each one a different name.

to crash and burn in the 1919 Black Sox scandal, he was famous as one of baseball's finest hitters—perhaps second only to Ty Cobb. Jackson had special treatments for his bats based on the time of year: During the season he rubbed his bats with sweet oil and wrapped them in a clean cotton cloth; each winter, he took his lumber home to Greenville, S.C., to shelter them from the cold Northern climes. "Bats don't like to freeze no more than me," he said.

Of course, special treatment may have been justified—one of Jackson's bats was possibly the most famous of any in baseball. Jackson called his bat "Black Betsy," originally made for him when he was a teenager living in South Carolina. The story is that Charlie Ferguson, a mechanic at the mill where Jackson worked, fashioned the bat. Jackson's baseball exploits had made him a local hero, and Ferguson made the young man a massive bat out of unseasoned hickory.

It's uncertain how the bat was darkened, although it's typically attributed to Jackson's spitting of tobacco juice on the bat and regularly soaking it in sweet oil. But Mike Nola, historian for the Shoeless Joe Jackson's Virtual Hall of Fame website, tried the spitting-and-rubbing technique and could not get a bat to come out anywhere near as dark as Jackson's, leading him to speculate that Jackson may have mixed dirt or clay with the oil. According to legend, upon arriving in the majors for a five-game stint in 1908 Jackson had the Spalding company trim Black Betsy down significantly from its original 48 ounces. (Some sources say it was cut to 39 ounces; and it is definitely true that later in the majors Shoeloess Joes switched to Louisville Sluggers that weighed 39 ounces.) Jackson went on to use a variety of sticks throughout his career and gave each its own name (The General, Dixie, Big Jim, and even Blonde Betsy, an unstained version of the original). As Shoeless Joe's career took off, fans began referring to every Jackson bat as "Black Betsy," cheering for it nearly as much as for him and giving his lumber a lasting identity in baseball history.

Jackson wasn't the only player to think a little color helped give his bat that something special. Harry "The Hat" Walker, the 1947 National League batting champion, loved hitting. And when he wasn't hitting, he was talking hitting. So it made sense that in his spare time, The Hat visited the Louisville Slugger factory. While there, Walker once saw a bat resting in the staining vat;

not realizing it was there merely to stir the liquid, Walker lifted it out and gave it the once-over. The bat—which was half-stained and half-natural from the way it was propped up in the vat—felt good in his hands, so Walker started ordering two-toned bats. Today, those bats are still said to have the "Walker Finish."

The "Foster Finish," by contrast, was created by design. In the 1970s, Cincinnati slugger George Foster reasoned that during night games an outfielder would have trouble picking up the ball off a dark bat. So he requested a bat that was extremely dark brown—many people mistakenly have called it black—instead of the traditional wood stain. This theory soon found a following among such hitters as singles maestro Wade Boggs, and it was popular with the new bat companies that arose in the 1990s. The Rockies' Dante Bichette and other players also praised the dark bats because the ball left a mark, allowing hitters to see where they were making contact and enabling them to adjust their swings accordingly.

Photo Credit: National Baseball Hall of Fame

The Walker Finish, as Louisville Slugger's two-tone approach is called, is named for Harry the Hat Walker.

Pete Rose took this concept more seriously than any other player. In his book *Pete Rose on Hitting*, Charlie Hustle explained that he cleaned his bat with rubbing alcohol after each game so he could see where his contact point was. "I remember I was facing Craig Swan during my forty-four game hitting streak," he wrote. "I had reached thirty-eight games in a row. The first pitch of the game was a ball. Then Swan threw an inside fastball, and I fouled it back. I called time out and looked at the bat. The mark was about an inch down the handle from where it should have been. He was throwing harder than I had thought. So I choked up a little, trying to make the bat a little lighter. Swan again threw the same pitch inside, but this time I hit a line drive over the shortstop's head for a base hit. If I hadn't adjusted, it would have been another foul ball, and the count would have been [1] and 2."

For some players, though, their bat decisions remain largely based on aesthetics. Pittsburgh's Andy Van Slyke requested a rose-colored barrel and a natural handle; San Diego's Tony Gwynn preferred a black barrel and a natural handle; and Derek Jeter orders a special hand-dipping treatment for a gold embossing on his bats.

While Rose applied cold logic to his choices and Jeter based his on looks, many players are less rational and driven more by superstition. Orlando Cepeda won a National League homer crown as a Giant and an MVP award as a Cardinal, but he didn't collect bats as much as he disposed of them. Cepeda often discarded a bat after getting a single hit for fear it had used up its allotment. "One year, we sent him more bats than we sent to some minor league teams," Louisville Slugger staffer Rex Bradley recalls.

The great Pirate slugger Willie Stargell was neither picky nor protective. His only stipulation was that the model he used had someone else's name on it! For example, Pops swung a Manny Sanguillen model in the 1979 World Series. But most ballplayers are far more territorial.

Joe Orsulak and Mark Grace were among players who threw bats away if they caught a pitcher touching them. "Pitchers suck all the hits out of bats," Grace explained. Wade Boggs was even more strict. When fellow infielder Mike Gallego picked up one of his game bats in the clubhouse to test it, Boggs grabbed it back, broke it in half, and dumped it; then he grabbed his other game bat and left. Albert Belle, who, not surprisingly, didn't like to share, wrapped each bat in a sanitary sock. Other players through the years had used this practice, but Belle tied his with a complicated knot so he could tell if anyone had opened it.

But when it comes to reacting badly to someone messing with his bat, perhaps no one has ever overreacted more passionately than Boston Brave first baseman Earl Torgeson (The Earl of Snohomish). On July 1, 1952, at Braves Field, Torgeson and New York Giants catcher Sal Yvars were bickering like brothers in the backseat on a long drive. Stop hitting me with your backswing, complained Yvars. No, it's your fault, snarled Torgeson, you have to move back because you're crowding the hitters. Back and forth they went until Torgeson seemingly ended the argument by smacking a single. In frustration, Yvars grabbed Torgeson's bat by the barrel and slammed it on home plate, breaking it. Torgeson was on base at the time so he didn't realize what had happened. But in the next inning word got back to him and—to the great surprise of everyone in the stands—Torgeson suddenly took off like a shot for the Giants' dugout, where he hauled off and punched Yvars in the eye, inciting a bench-clearing brawl. Torgeson was ejected from the game, while Yvars needed three stitches. The bad feelings over the broken bat lingered, and two years later the two players got into another on-field fight.

Hitters are always quirky and superstitious about their bats, but never more so than when things are going especially well or especially badly. They will try anything to break out of a slump, for example. Through the first four games of 1971, Johnny Bench, the National League's defending home run and runs-batted-in champion, had zero homers and no RBI. Furthermore, the Reds were 0-4. Teammate Tommy Helms suggested that Bench switch bats—it's a time-honored baseball tradition to blame a slump on the bat, not the person swinging it. Needing a slump-buster, Bench grabbed a bat that a fan had given him in spring training—it was dressed up with red velvet on the handle. The Little General hammered four homers in the next three games, leading Cincinnati to a sweep of the Braves.

Most players aren't Johnny Bench, of course, so they may require a more legitimate solution. One day, catcher Jason Kendall, then with Pittsburgh, found one thanks to a friend, Pirates equipment manager Roger Wilson. "He came to me and said, 'I need some help, I need you to give some luck to my bat,'" Wilson recalled. When Kendall went to the plate that day, there was a message near the barrel of the bat. "See the ball, hit the ball," Wilson's handwritten advice said. Kendall felt relaxed and did just that, pounding out a couple of hits and then going on a two-week hitting spree. Some of Kendall's teammates kiddingly asked Wilson for messages of their own, and Wilson responded by drawing a big black X on their bats.

After Kendall broke his lucky bat, he sought out Wilson for more messages—and got them, although not all were directly related to baseball. Wilson would write a line from a movie they had discussed, or something from everyday life that could be connected to the game. Sometimes it was even a one-word note, like "knocks," which is slang for hits. Those short ones might be on the knob instead of the barrel. "The idea was that when he got to the plate and read it, [the message] would clear his head from all other thoughts," Wilson said. "It would help him focus."

In 2005, Adam Dunn had the folks at Louisville Slugger actually etch a message into his bat to break an odd sort of slump. Dunn had gone 1,000 plate appearances without collecting a sacrifice fly, so he had his bat inscribed with the words "Sac Fly." He broke the drought with two that year. (Pitcher A.J. Burnett, before he moved to the American League, where he didn't need many more bats, made the most unusual requests for his bats, replacing his name with those of his favorite rock stars like Kid Rock and Marilyn Manson.)

Another remedy for slumps employed by a catcher came from catcher Terry Steinbach, who ordered his lumber from two different bat-makers. When he stopped hitting with one manufacturer's product, he switched to the other company's bats until they no longer "worked," and then he went back to the first bats in an attempt to find those elusive hits.

Other slumping-breaking stories abound, some more believable than others: Pitchers Bill Caudill and Dock Ellis helped their teams break batting slumps by burning their own bats; Jim Fregosi once asked a team doctor for a cortisone shot for his bat, then hit for the cycle; a catcher in the Phillies' farm system, mired in a slump, drew eyes and a pair of glasses on the barrel of his bat and proceeded to blast two homers. The most outlandish of these (perhaps apocryphal) stories recalls an unnamed Reds coach who once called the bat-maker of the Louisville Slugger, Hillerich & Bradsby, questioning the merit of his team's bats. The person he reached supposedly recommended roasting the bats in front of the dugout for one hour on each side—and the foolish/desperate coach did just that. And, the story goes, the Reds got red-hot immediately afterwards.

Chapter 3

THE REAL WONDERBOYS
Glorious deeds accomplished with bat in hand

I don't believe...what I just saw!
I don't *believe* what I just saw!

Jack Buck on CBS Radio
with the call of Kirk Gibson's walkoff home run
to end Game 1 of the 1988 World Series

A man, a bat, a nickname for the ages, 1911

In the dead-ball era, the home run rarely took center stage...until the 1911 World Series.

Frank Baker, the third baseman in the Philadelphia Athletics slick-fielding, strong-hitting, "$100,000 Infield," was a perfect example of baseball hitters back then. In 1911, he smacked 14 triples, yet he finished only sixth in the league in triples; he managed only 11 four-baggers, but that was enough to win him his first of four straight home run crowns. (He hit a grand total of 42 over those four years.)

Baker used a short, thick-handled bat that Jack McGrath of Louisville Slugger once said—presumably with a serious dose of exaggeration on the weight—was "antiquated even in its time. The handle was almost the size of the barrel. It was short, but almost like a piece of lead, because it weighed over fifty ounces. There was no flex. It really was a wagon tongue."

Baker supposedly rubbed his heavy war club with a magical mix of secret ingredients. Whether this was true or not, he could really swing the stick, and New York Giants manager John McGraw warned his pitchers about throwing fastballs up and in to Baker in the World Series. Giants legend Christy Mathewson shut down the A's in Game 1, but Baker had two hits and scored Philadelphia's lone run.

In Game 2, the Giants Rube Marquard yielded a first-inning run but then

35

retired 13 consecutive batters until Eddie Collins roped a sixth-inning double. Up came Baker. Marquard challenged him with a fastball up and in, and Baker slammed it over the right field wall. The A's won, 3-1.

The next day, a nationally syndicated column appeared under Mathewson's byline that ripped Marquard: "There was no excuse for it. [We] knew what pitches were difficult for him to hit, and those he could hit for extra bases. Well, Rube threw him the kind of ball that Baker likes."

Photo Credit: Library of Congress, LC-DIG-ggbain-09859

Frank "Home Run" Baker used a short, stiff and thick bat, which a Louisville Slugger employee once said "was antiquated even in its time."

Because Mathewson was baseball's golden boy at the time, the upstanding citizen among immigrants and ruffians, the column, in which he aired dirty team laundry in public, stirred national controversy.

The drama escalated in Game 3 when Baker produced a follow-up that seemed straight out of a morality play. Mathewson pitched superbly through eight innings, holding Baker hitless in three at-bats and leading, 1-0. Then Baker came up with one out in the ninth. Despite everything he'd written, Mathewson threw a pitch in virtually the same location as Marquard's home run ball—with the same result. Baker launched a drive into the right field stands, tying the game at 1-1.

Baker also made a clutch defensive play in the 10th and singled during Philadelphia's winning two-run breakthrough in the 11th inning, but it was the homer that captured headlines and the public imagination. The next day, Mathewson ate crow in print; meanwhile, a ghost-written column with Marquard's byline snapped back at his teammate.

As the clubs waited out six days of rain before Game 4, the only baseball story people talked about was the feud of two star pitchers and the man behind it all. In the end, the A's won the Series and Frank Baker had a new nickname, one for the ages: Home Run Baker.

Ruth carves out his place in history, 1927

Babe Ruth liked to make his mark in baseball. With certain bats, when the Sultan of Swat swatted another long ball, he'd carve a notch around the Louisville Slugger logo. And in 1927, Ruth carved more notches than anyone could have imagined when he broke his own single-season record by walloping 60 home runs.

Ruth used bats of varying weights throughout his career, but at the beginning of that celebrated season he approached the bat-makers at Louisville Slugger and asked for a new model—one in the style used by retired Tigers star Sam Crawford, only the Babe wanted his bats an inch longer—a 35-inch, 38-ounce, R43 model.

Photo Credit: Louisville Slugger Museum & Factory

Babe Ruth made marks on his bats, carving a notch for each home run he swatted with this stick in 1927.

Ruth had set the home run record in 1919 with 29, broken that mark in 1920 with 54, and rewritten the record book again in 1921 with 59. In 1927, with many sports heroes of the early 1920s—Red Grange, Bill Tilden, and Jack Dempsey included—starting to fade, the 32-year-old Ruth was determined to show that he was a unique talent.

All season long he battled his teammate, an up-and-coming youngster named Lou Gehrig, for the lead in homers. In September the veteran left the youth behind, but after 151 games Ruth was sitting on 56 homers and chances of breaking his own mark of 59 seemed remote (although the Yankees would play 155 games that year—one more than scheduled—because of an early-season tie).

Then Ruth struck. He walloped a grand slam off Lefty Grove for his 57th homer (no other American League *team* topped 56 in 1927). In his next game he hit a solo home run and another bases-full shot. He had tied his record, riveting fans across the nation. On September 30, in the next-to-last game of the season, Ruth faced Washington Senators lefthander Tom Zachary at Yankee Stadium. Ruth had torched him twice that year, so Zachary decided to pitch around the Bambino. The fans rode him for walking Ruth on four pitches in the first inning, but Zachary continued nibbling. Ruth managed singles his next two times up, scoring both times, and the game was tied 2-2 in the eighth when Ruth came up with a runner on third and Gehrig and Bob Meusel up next.

With the game on the line, Zachary no longer had his wiggle room. He didn't want to walk Ruth to face Gehrig in this situation. On a 1-1 pitch, Zachary threw a curve inside and at the knees—"as good as any I ever threw," he recalled later—but Ruth read it perfectly and yanked the ball into the right field bleachers. The fans tossed "Homer 60" hats in the air and shredded paper to create instant confetti as Ruth toured the bases.

Afterward, the Babe offered a challenge that no one would meet in the history of the 154-game schedule: "Sixty, count 'em, sixty! Let's see some other son of a bitch match that!"

The Hall of Fame has the R43 he used on that fateful day, but the Louisville Slugger Museum & Factory has its own special display—the bat the Babe used to swat 21 of his round-trippers that year, with a notch for each one circling around the logo.

Joe D, with a little help from his friends, 1941

The nation's eyes were on Joe DiMaggio in 1941 when he mounted a challenge to George Sisler's modern record of hitting safely in 41 consecutive games and Wee Willie Keeler's all-time mark of 44. On June 29 at Washington's Griffith Stadium, Joltin' Joe had a chance to tie and break Sisler's record in a doubleheader against the Senators.

DiMaggio fouled out on a 3-0 count in the fourth inning of the opener—the Yankee Clipper was grateful for getting the green light from manager Joe McCarthy—but he smacked a double in the sixth inning to tie Sisler.

But while DiMaggio and the Yankees were celebrating in the clubhouse between games, someone sneaked into the dugout and stole DiMaggio's Louisville Slugger D-29, the 36-inch, 36-ounce bat (minus the half-ounce that Joe had personally sandpapered off at the handle).

DiMaggio was distraught. Like so many ballplayers, he was superstitious. Besides, that bat handle had been perfectly tapered. Taking a new bat, he went hitless his first three times up in the nightcap. The streak was in peril. But Tommy Henrich, who had been swinging a bat he'd borrowed from the great man back in June, persuaded DiMaggio to try the familiar old stick. In the seventh, DiMaggio singled to left. He had made history.

Photo credit: National Baseball Hall of Fame

Still, DiMaggio wanted his lucky lumber back. What happened next is shrouded in myth and mystery. DiMaggio supposedly asked radio announcer Mel Allen to make an over-the-air offer of six new bats in exchange

Everyone associates Joe DiMaggio with the number 56, but during his heralded hitting streak the "magic number" was 45—one more than Wee Willie Keeler's consecutive game record. After setting that new mark, the Yankee Clipper posed for this special picture. He then went on to hit in 11 more consecutive games.

for the original, hoping just maybe the thief would hear of the offer and make the trade. But DiMaggio also went to two street-smart friends (one a low-level racketeer) and asked them to track down the culprit and retrieve the missing bat. The bat eventually wound up back in DiMaggio's hands, although the story varied from telling to telling—either the thief heard DiMaggio's public plea and felt bad, or he returned the bat in exchange for cash or Yankees tickets, or perhaps he gave it up, shall we say, under duress.

With his prized bat back, DiMaggio autographed the one that Henrich had handed him to break the modern record, with that bat being auctioned off to raise money for the USO. DiMaggio's status was enhanced even more when his streak surpassed Keeler's mark on July 2, and then the Yankee Clipper permanently entered the ranks of the all-time greats when he reached an unfathomable 56 games on July 14, 1941, before finally having his streak snapped. That record has never been seriously threatened.

Williams' fabulous finish, 1941

All season long, even as Joe DiMaggio had wowed America with his 56-game hitting streak, Ted Williams had kept his batting average in the stratosphere, well above .400. No one had come close to that mark since Bill Terry hit .401 in 1930, and baseball people were beginning to wonder if there'd ever be another .400 hitter.

Then, be it pressure or fatigue or the laws of nature, Williams hit a skid, going 3-for-14 over four games, slicing six points off his average. And so it was that with one double-header left in the season, Williams' average had fallen to exactly .39955.

Williams could have sat out the doubleheader and that number would have been rounded off; the record books would have shown that the great Boston slugger had hit .400 for the year. But Williams would have known that he had cut a critical corner. So he insisted on being in the starting lineup in two otherwise meaningless games.

In the first game, he singled and homered off rookie Dick Fowler and singled twice against lefty reliever Porter Vaughan. His 4-for-5 performance left his average at .4039. He had proven himself worthy of the claim, so surely he would sit out the second game, right? Not Williams. Putting his accomplishment back on the line, Williams banged a single and a double in three at-bats, raising his average to .406.

When the game ended, fans charged the field and headed for Williams. His first reaction was to grab his bat before anyone else could. In the dugout afterwards, Williams, who rarely showed his effusive side in public, posed kissing his lumber in joyous celebration.

The Giants win the pennant! 1951

Bottom of the ninth, one out, New York Giants runners on second and third and a two-run difference in the winner-take-all third game of the 1951 National League playoff series to decide the most dramatic pennant race of all-time.

After blowing a 13½-game August lead, needing a tense 14-inning victory on the final day of the regular season to force the playoff, and then losing the opening game of the pennant-deciding series to the Giants before tying the series, the Brooklyn Dodgers now stood just two outs from redemption and the World Series. Although one run was already in during the bottom of the ninth, the Dodgers still had a 4-2 lead. But standing in their way was a Giant with a bat, Bobby Thomson,

Photo Credit: National Baseball Hall of Fame

Bobby Thomson's Shot Heard Round the World is probably baseball's most celebrated home run in baseball history, and the bat Thomson used to smash it has achieved iconic stature.

wielding a 35-inch Adirondack 302, sold to him by former teammate-turned-bat salesman Hal Schumacher.

Ralph Branca, the new Giants pitcher, knew Thompson well. Thompson had already clubbed 31 home runs that year, including two off Branca in the regular season and another in Game 1 of the playoff series. But the Dodgers chose not to walk Thompson and put the winning run on base. Branca fired a fastball for a strike. Then he tried another heater, high and tight, to set Thompson up for his next pitch. But this one was neither high enough nor tight enough. Thompson's Adirondack sliced through the air. The crack of wood on ball echoed through the Polo Grounds and into history. A hard, spinning liner headed toward the left field wall, just 315 feet away. Dodgers left fielder Andy Pafko thought the ball might bounce off the wall, but he looked up…and announcer Russ Hodges famously shouted into his microphone: "It's gonna be, I believe. The Giants win the pennant! The Giants win the pennant! The Giants win the pennant! The Giants win the pennant! Bobby Thomson hits into the lower deck of the left field stands. The Giants win the pennant!

And they're going crazy. They're going crazy…!"

The ball disappeared into the afternoon, never to be seen again, its mysterious departure eventually forming the foundation of Don DeLillo's novel, *Underworld*. It became The Shot Heard Round the World. But someone brought Thomson the bat in the clubhouse—he didn't remember exactly how he got it back—and he donated it to the Hall of Fame. The bat held such magical power in the American psyche that, to Thomson's amazement, it frequently traveled the country in exhibits—it was present, for instance, at the opening of Bob Feller's museum in Iowa. "I went to that one with Ralph Branca," Thomson said not long before his death, "but sometimes they just send the bat."

Mantle's 565-footer, 1953

Loren Babe had a great baseball name, but in his brief stint with the Yankees—12 games in 1952 and five in 1953—the infielder didn't hit a single homer for New York. Babe's bat however, fulfilled his name's destiny in the hands of a true Yankee slugger, Mickey Mantle.

On April 17, 1953, at Griffith Stadium, the Mick grabbed one of Babe's bats in the fifth inning as he went to hit against Washington lefthander Chuck Stobbs. Mantle, still struggling to emerge from Joe DiMaggio's shadow, took one giant stride that afternoon when he rocketed a pitch over the fence in left-center, 391 feet from the plate; the shot carried to a back wall, another 69 feet away. Atop that 50-foot wall was a scoreboard, off which the ball glanced before disappearing.

Yankees publicist Red Patterson told reporters he'd found the ball in the backyard of a house and that he'd paced off the carry of the ball at an astonishing 565 feet. That whopping distance was a bit of a whopper in itself, though. Although a 10-year-old boy found the ball, it had, in reality, rolled into the yard. And while the smash became famous as the first "tape measure" home run, Patterson hadn't actually measured it—he'd simply made up the number. Some historians believe the homer traveled 510 feet on the fly. Still, thanks to Babe—who wound up playing most of the season with the Philadelphia Athletics (for whom he hit his only two major league homers)—Mantle had given birth to the Tale of the Tape.

Ten years later, Mantle hit an even more impressive shot—and again did it with a borrowed bat. This one belonged to Dale Long, who at least had genuine power. On May 22, 1963, against the Kansas City A's, Mantle won a game in the 11th inning when he crushed a Bill Fischer pitch so hard it was still rising when it struck the top of the right field facade atop Yankee Stadium. A physicist estimated that had it cleared the roof, it would have traveled 620 feet. Mantle said it was his hardest-hit ball ever, and he told Long it was the only time "the bat actually bent in my hands."

The greatest clutch homer ever forgotten, 1960

Down to the bitter end—the ninth inning of the seventh game—the New York Yankees believed they would outslug the Pittsburgh Pirates in the 1960 World Series. In the first six games, the Pirates had pulled out 6-4, 3-2, and 5-2 victories, but the Yankees had bombarded the Bucs 16-3, 10-0, and 12-0. New York had outscored Pittsburgh overall 46-17, outhit them 78-49, and outhomered them 8-1. The only player to homer for Pittsburgh in the first six games certainly wasn't a Mantle or Maris, it was slick-fielding second baseman Bill Mazeroski, who had hit one out back in Game 1.

Game 7 looked to be more of the same Yankee blowout as the Bronx Bombers stormed back from a 4-0 deficit to grab a 7-4 lead thanks to homers from Moose Skowron and Yogi Berra. Forbes Field fans knew they were only six outs from watching New York stroll off with the eighth championship of the Casey Stengel era. But fate grabbed the Yankees by the throat in the Pirates' eighth when Bill Virdon's sure double-play grounder took a bad hop and hit shortstop Tony Kubek in the larynx. Kubek was unable to make a play on the ball—indeed, he was forced to leave the game—and Pittsburgh had the break it needed. Singles by Dick Groat and then two outs later by Roberto Clemente cut the Pirates' deficit to 7-6.

With two on and two out in the eighth, the batter was back-up catcher Hal Smith, a former Yankees farmhand who had entered the game in the top half of the inning. He had good pop—he'd hit 11 homers in just 286 at-bats in 1960—but he had just two singles in seven at-bats in the Series. Smith was toting a 34½-inch, 32-ounce Louisville Slugger, a Stan Musial model, with plenty of rosin on the handle.

Smith took a big rip at a fastball from Yankee reliever Jim Coates and missed. Behind 1-2, however, he got another fastball and this time he connected, drilling a three-run homer. Forbes Field erupted with joy and Smith was mobbed by his jubilant teammates in the dugout. Pittsburgh had a stunning 9-7 lead. "We thought we had it won," Smith recalled more than a half-century later.

But the Yankees offense refused to quit, and they scrapped back in the top of the ninth to tie the score at 9-9.

The deadlock was short-lived, however. On Ralph Terry's second pitch in the bottom of the ninth, Mazeroski, who had also hit 11 home runs in the regular season (although in a lot more at-bats than Smith), smashed a homer to left, setting off delirium at old Forbes Field.

Mazeroski became a World Series hero and Hall of Famer, while Smith's shot was reduced to being perhaps the most overlooked clutch hit in baseball history. "I guess I wasn't meant to be a hero," Smith says, but he points out that he did some things—hitting a World Series homer and winning a crown—that most players, "even Ted Williams, never got to do."

While Mazeroski's and Smith's paths diverged, their bats met identical fates, Smith says. "Our owner [John Galbreath] came and took the bats and the uniforms. I think he kept them for himself."

Smith contented himself with a special black World Series bat with engraved autographs of all his teammates, a souvenir he has since passed down to his children.

Maris' 61 in 162. 1961

After the Yankees' 27th game in 1961, reigning American League MVP Roger Maris had only three homers. Teammate Mickey Mantle had 10. But Maris smashed 23 in his next 36 games, and the greatest home run race since Babe Ruth and Lou Gehrig went at it in 1927 was on.

Entering play on July 17, with Maris at 35 homers and Mantle at 32, commissioner Ford Frick, a former ghost-writer for and buddy of Ruth, declared that the new 162-game schedule implemented because of expansion meant that a player would not officially break Ruth's single-season home run record of 60 unless he topped the coveted number in 154 games. Most sportswriters and players supported Frick's edict—Mantle himself said, "If I should break it in the 155th game, I wouldn't want the record."

Maris retorted, "A season's a season." Then he faced down the horrific pressure piled on by the fans and the media, most of whom were rooting either for Ruth's ghost or for Mantle. Maris kept on homering, even after he lost the protection of Mantle in the lineup (and in the clubhouse) when the center fielder went down with injuries in September. Still, Maris fell short. He hit his 59th home run in the Yankees' 154th game played to a decision—their 155th overall, considering a tie game in April. He hit No. 60 off Baltimore's Jack Fisher in New York's 159th game overall, then sat out the next game and failed to homer in the ensuing two games. That left only the season finale for Maris to surpass Ruth's figure.

Only 23,154 fans showed up at Yankee Stadium on October 1. Maris was retired on a fly ball to left field in the first inning, but in his second at-bat—in the fourth inning— Red Sox pitcher Tracy Stallard left a 2-0 pitch out over the plate and the New York slugger's 35-inch, 33-ounce bat sent the ball on an arc into the right field stands. It proved to be the only run of the game.

Afterward, Maris looked at his Louisville Slugger and said, "I don't imagine I'll be using this bat again." Indeed, while Maris himself never made it to the Hall of Fame, the bat used to hit No. 61 earned that prized honor.

It was briefly retrieved in 1998 for his sons Randy, Kevin, and Rich to

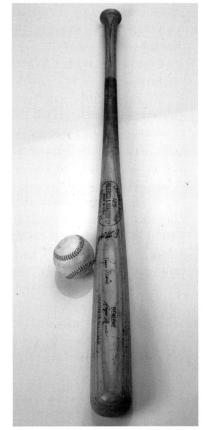

Photo Credit: National Baseball Hall of Fame

Sure, Roger Maris needed 162 games to break Babe Ruth's 154-game mark, but he didn't need andro, the "cream and the clear," or other artificial boosters. Just his trusty Louisville Slugger.

hold and cherish in St. Louis when Mark McGwire broke their father's record. But these days, given what we know (or don't know) about McGwire, Sammy Sosa, and Barry Bonds (the only three who have hit more than 61 home runs in a season) it seems likely that only Roger Maris, the pride of Fargo, North Dakota, set that mark armed only with the bat in his hands.

Blomberg, the first DH, 1973

Injuries prevented Ron Blomberg from living up to his potential as the first overall pick in the June amateur draft in 1967, but he did end up with one of his bats on display at the Hall of Fame…albeit a bat that never put a ball in play during a game.

Baseball has always been conflicted about the designated hitter—the DH—an American League innovation intended to add offense by creating a position for hitting-proficient players who might not be adept in the field and allowing light-hitting pitchers to skip their trips to the plate. And this odd commemoration of the DH's debut is a perfect reflection of that.

Of the American League opening-day games in 1973, the first year of the DH, the Yankees-Red Sox game at Fenway Park had the earliest start—so New York's Blomberg was the first DH in major league history. He had been presumed to be the starting first baseman but was switched to DH by manager Ralph Houk on the eve of the game to get Felipe Alou's bat into the lineup. Boston's Orlando Cepeda would be the second DH ever to bat. Cepeda would reach the Hall on his own merits, but on this day he would go 0-for-6 and contribute nothing to Boston's 15-5 rout.

Blomberg toted a 38-inch, 37-ounce Louisville Slugger (model R161) to the plate, a heavy piece of lumber that he said "helped make me work my hands and be quicker with them."

Blomberg had learned to take care of his bats as a boy when his parents had little money for extra equipment and he was known for lugging his bats everywhere so no one else would use them. "My bat was like a little baby," said Blomberg, who as one of the game's few Jewish players put a Jewish star on the handle of his game bats. "And I made darn sure they were well taken care of."

When Blomberg, who batted .293 over eight major league seasons, made DH history in the first inning, the situation was certainly propitious. The Yankees had loaded the bases against Luis Tiant with two out, thanks to a double and two walks. Blomberg drove home a run, but he didn't put that hefty bat to use—Tiant walked him too.

"See, the DH has added offense to the game already," quipped Matty Alou, the man who trotted in from third base.

But Yankees publicist Marty Appel, an astute student of baseball history, knew that the bat from the first trip to the plate of any DH was special, and he raced into the clubhouse and had the clubhouse man take the stick away from Blomberg to be shipped off to the Hall of Fame.

It was a good move too—for while that bat went, dent-free, to Cooperstown, Blomberg managed a single later in the game but shattered his bat—the first hit for a DH in history—in the process. "They probably just threw that one away," Blomberg laughs.

Aaron's 715th, 1974

On the night of April 8, 1974, Hank Aaron faced off against the Dodgers Al Downing in front of the largest crowd (53,775) in Atlanta history. When Aaron had started playing baseball, he didn't know how to hold a bat, swinging cross-handed. When he first made his mark with the Braves, he did so by swinging bats made for others—a Del Crandall-model Louisville Slugger, for example. But Aaron quietly and steadily became his own man, albeit with an echo of the most renowned home run hitter of all-time. The A99 model that Aaron used in April 1974 was similarly proportioned to the R43 swung by none other than Babe Ruth, although Aaron's bat—35 inches and 33 ounces— was significantly lighter.

Aaron walked his first time up, in the second inning, and came around to score his 2,063rd run, breaking Willie Mays' National League record in that category. But on his second time up, in the fourth inning, Hammerin' Hank broke a far more momentous record when he cracked Downing's 1-0 pitch 385 feet over the fence in left-centerfield. It was home run number 715 and Aaron had finally surpassed Ruth to become baseball's all-time home run king. (Braves relief pitcher Tom House caught the ball in the bullpen). Los Angeles infielders Davey Lopes and Bill Russell congratulated Aaron as he trotted around the bases, and fans rushed onto the field to be near him. Aaron, who had endured withering attacks and threats throughout the record chase, then basked in an outpouring of affection from his family and the fans during an 11-minute celebration of the historic moment.

Carbo sets the stage for Fisk, 1975

Mention the 1975 World Series and any baseball fan will immediately see Carlton Fisk waving his Game 6 home run fair. But while Fisk's 12th-inning home run is among baseball's most famous, the entire World Series would have been over before that if not for another oft-overlooked home run.

Pudge's Boston Red Sox were trailing the Cincinnati Reds 3 games to 2 in the Series and were down 6-3 in the eighth inning when manager Darrell Johnson turned to Bernie Carbo. Now, Fisk was not just an All-Star, he was a hard-working New Englander, who was essentially the living symbol of Red Sox Nation. Carbo was the opposite, an ex-Cincinnati Red whose career was foundering because he was wallowing in drug and alcohol abuse. (Carbo finally cleaned up his life in the 1990s.)

Carbo had already missed batting practice during an off day in the series because he claimed he couldn't find Tufts University, where the team was meeting. Then, in the hours leading up to his at-bat, he confessed decades later, "I probably smoked two joints, drank about three or four beers, got to the ballpark, took some [amphetamines], took a pain pill, drank a cup of coffee, chewed some tobacco, had a cigarette."

Stuck riding the pine, Carbo whiled away the early innings of the game fiddling with his Louisville Slugger. He smoothed and sanded it so much he took all the polish off and, he later said, even eradicated the logo. Teammate Rick Wise reportedly told him he wouldn't be allowed to use the bat like that, so Carbo wrote the words "Louisville Slugger" on the bat in magic marker. "That's how I kept myself amused," he said.

With two outs and two on in the eighth, Johnson told Carbo he was pinch-hitting for the pitcher, but Carbo was convinced that Cincinnati manager Sparky Anderson would bring in a lefty to face him, which would in turn prompt Johnson to replace him with Juan Beniquez. But Anderson left pitcher Rawly Eastwick in and Carbo was not mentally prepared on the first two pitches, which zipped by him for called strikes. Fortunately for Red Sox fans, Eastwick then twice missed the strike zone.

With the count now even, Carbo finally took a hack—an awful swing that catcher Johnny Bench reportedly said looked like a Little Leaguer just learning how to hit—but he'd gotten more of the ball than he thought on his freshly whittled bat and it sailed out of the park for one of the most stunning pinch-hit homers in World Series history. Three innings later, of course, Carbo and his bat were overshadowed by Fisk and his dance.

Reggie, Reggie, Reggie, 1977

In 1977, Reggie Jackson was not just a fearsome slugger. He also was a magnet for attention and controversy. From his first days in a Yankees uniform, Jackson ("I didn't come to New York to become a star, I brought my star with me") stirred up conflicts with manager Billy Martin, teammate Thurman Munson, and others. Some of it was his doing, some wasn't, but in the end Jackson made it all worthwhile.

His landmark achievement came in Game 6 of the World Series against the Los Angeles Dodgers, when he became the first person since Babe Ruth to smash three home runs in a World Series game, single-handedly bringing the Yankees their first crown in 15 seasons.

Jackson's three homers came on just three swings off three different pitchers (Burt Hooten, Elias Sosa, and Charlie Hough). He had lived up to his own hype.

And then, of course, another controversy broke out: In the November 19th issue of *The Sporting News*, the Hillerich & Bradsby bat company took out a full-page ad congratulating Jackson on his achievement; the ad showed Jackson's J93 Louisville Slugger (but not Jackson swinging it) and called him a "member of the Louisville Slugger Advisory Staff."

This all seemed innocent enough. But three weeks later, Rawlings, maker of Adirondack's Big Stick, launched an ad of its own: "H&B…How do you sleep at night? Doesn't it bother you just a little to capitalize on Reggie's glory, when he set all those World Series slugging records with an Adirondack bat? It bothers us."

And there, on the page, Rawlings ran the original H&B ad and also showed a dramatic picture of Jackson in mid-swing in Game 6, using a bat with the distinctive Adirondack Pro Ring just above the handle.

The reality is even murkier. Jackson did have a contract with Hillerich & Bradsby, but he frequently used an Adirondack Big Stick. Furthermore, it was reported that Jackson occasionally would paint the black Adirondack ring on his Louisville Sluggers. So Mr. October might indeed have been using the kind of bat that Hillerich & Bradsby boasted about.

This kind of subterfuge is not totally unheard of among sluggers. Philadelphia's Mike Schmidt, another member with Jackson of the 500-homer club, once proudly declared that he was perhaps the only player to reach that plateau after spending a career exclusively using Adirondacks. But then in his next breath, he confessed, "And even if I ever did love to use a Louisville Slugger bat, I'd at least tape a red ring on it so it looked like an Adirondack."

Dent jolts Red Sox, 1978

After 162 games, there was no daylight between the New York Yankees and the Boston Red Sox in the 1978 American League East Division race. The Yankees had stormed back from 14 games down to capture first place in September, only to have the Red Sox recover with an eight-game winning streak that caught the Yankees on the season's final day. In the archrivals' tense one-game playoff, the Sox took a 2-0 lead into the seventh inning at Fenway Park. Boston fans thought they could finally see the light between the teams.

But after two one-out singles, New York manager Bob Lemon had Jim Spencer pinch-hit for back-up second baseman Brian Doyle. If starter Willie Randolph were not injured, Lemon would have saved Spencer for the next batter, weak-hitting shortstop Bucky Dent. But Spencer flied out and Dent got his shot.

Dent, a .243 hitter, was in an 0-for-13 rut. When he fell behind 0-2 Red Sox pitcher Mike Torrez seemed poised to escape the jam. But on that second strike, Dent fouled the pitch off his foot and hopped away from the plate in pain, giving fate—a.k.a., Yankee outfielder Mickey Rivers—a chance to intervene. During batting practice, Rivers had noticed that the Roy White model bat that he and Dent were both using was chipped, so he got a duplicate. Now he noticed Dent was still using the injured bat, so Rivers foisted the new edition into Dent's hands.

Meanwhile, Torrez failed to take warm-up pitches during the delay and lost his rhythm so his 0-2 waste pitch instead floated fat over the plate. Dent lifted a fly to left. Even with the new bat he didn't get much on it, but in Boston the Green Monster was just 315 feet away. So instead of making a long, forgotten out, Dent had a short, devastating, and very memorable three-run homer. New York had the lead and this one they would not relinquish, breaking the Red Sox nation's heart once again.

Rose surpasses Cobb, 1985

In his playing days, Pete Rose—relentless, overachieving, and self-mythologizing—was as All-American as can be. His bats, however, were not. During his career, Rose switched from Louisville Slugger to a black Mizuno bat handcrafted in Japan by the company's top master, Isokazu Kubota. (Charlie Hustle reportedly sent Kubota a favorite bat, then the bat-maker tapped it on the floor and listened to it to better help him replicate what Rose wanted.) Afraid of being criticized for this foreign "outsourcing," Rose, a flag-on-his-sleeve type, defended himself by claiming "the tree (Mizuno used) was from Louisville." (This was absurd because even Louisville Slugger doesn't get its wood from Louisville.)

Some of Rose's Mizuno bats were stolen for resale, so Rose always kept them near him on the field during warm-ups and locked them away in special trunks when the team was traveling. In 1985 there were reports that Rose used multiple bats in his chase of Ty Cobb's all-time hits record so he could sell them all off later. (Rose later went to prison for tax evasion that stemmed in part from cash reaped from memorabilia sales.) And, to top it all off, there were rumors, which still persist, that Rose was corking his bat to increase bat speed and make up for his slowing reflexes.

Still, on September 11, 1985, fifty-seven years to the day after Cobb's last at-bat, Rose got what he called "The Big Knock"—a single that broke the Georgia Peach's mark. Rose cried during the seven-minute ovation from his hometown Cincinnati crowd, but he was far less sentimental about the 34-inch, 32-ounce Mizuno with five circles of tape on the handle that he used to get record-breaking hit number 4,192. Paul Janzen, an alleged gambling partner, later claimed that Rose promised to pay off debts with money from selling the bat; and in fact Rose sold the bat along with the ball, reportedly for $125,000, to a man named Steve Wolter from Cincinnati, but he reportedly never paid up the money he owed to Janzen.

After he retired, Rose gave one of his black bats to his son, Pete Jr., who was called up by Cincinnati in 1997. In his debut, young Rose used his father's special lumber—and struck out. In his next at-bat, he switched to one of shortstop Barry Larkin's bats and managed a single—one of only two hits in his brief major league career.

Gibson's Series stunner, 1988

As the ninth inning of Game 1 of the 1988 World Series began, the action that mattered most was not on the field—where heavily favored Oakland led Los Angeles 4-3—but in the Dodgers' clubhouse, where determined grunts and pain-filled groans filled the air. Kirk Gibson, his hamstring so sore and his knee so banged up that he had watched the pregame introductions from the trainer's room, had told his wife to leave after seven innings to beat traffic because he couldn't play.

But now he had pulled on his uniform and was hitting the ball off a tee. Although a cane was more appropriate than a bat at that point, Gibson figured that if the Dodgers got the tying run on base, he'd grit his teeth through one at-bat.

On the field, manager Tommy Lasorda slyly seduced All-Star closer Dennis Eckersley into providing just that situation. With two men out and Dodgers pinch hitter Mike Davis at bat, Lasorda sent weak-hitting Dave Anderson to the on-deck circle to hit for pitcher Alejandro Pena, hiding Gibson at the end of the bench. Eckersley decided that Davis had too much power potential, so he pitched him away and issued what was for him a rare walk, figuring he'd blow away Anderson. But then Dodger Stadium exploded with noise. It wasn't Anderson heading to the plate. It was Gibson, who was coming off a season for which he would be accorded MVP honors.

Having put some tar and resin on his black-stained, 34-inch, 33-ounce Worth bat known as the Tennessee Thumper, Gibson hobbled forth to the plate. The bat, Gibson once noted in an interview, was like him—worn, but tough. "It's got a lot of tar on it, and where I hit my cleats the indentations are very deep," he said. "The paint's off where I fouled the balls off."

Eckersley immediately put Gibson in the hole 0-2, but the indefatigable hitter gamely fouled off a third heater and then ran the count full while Davis stole second base.

Needing only a single to tie the score, Gibson recalled the words of scout Mel Didier, who had told him of Eckersley, "Partner, as sure as I'm standing here breathing today, if you get to 3-and-2 he'll throw a back-door slider to you."

That's exactly what the future Hall of Fame reliever threw, and Gibson was ready. Although he had no strength in his legs, Gibson was able to wrist the ball into the right field stands for one of the most shocking home runs in World Series history.

Gibson didn't appear in the Series again, but a stunned Oakland team collapsed and the Dodgers prevailed in five games. Later, Gibson said of his bat, "You can see where I hit the home run. I chipped a piece of black paint off it, because the contact was so tough. It tells everything."

Carter's heroics, 1993

Philadelphia was on the verge of forcing a seventh game in the 1993 World Series, clinging to a 6-5 lead over Toronto in the ninth inning of Game 6. Phillies closer Mitch "Wild Thing" Williams came and quickly worked his way into a two-on, one-out jam. Up came outfielder Joe Carter, who had already smashed five homers over three years worth of post-season play for the Blue Jays. But Carter was hitless on the night and hitless in four previous tries against Williams. Williams fell behind 2-0 but came back with two quick strikes, the second of which had Carter looking awkward in his swing. Then the Phillies closer tried busting Carter inside with a fastball—Carter didn't even realize it was a fastball, calling it a slider afterward—and he turned on it, the ball zooming out and over the wall considerably faster than it had come in to the plate. Carter and the Jays had won back-to-back World Series, the first team to do so in 15 years. Carter was just the second player—Pittsburgh's Bill Mazeroski was the first, in 1960—to end a World Series with a home run, and he was the first to end a Series with a come-from-behind homer. He did it with a 35-inch, 32-ounce Louisville Slugger J93 model; this ash bat is now on display in the Hall of Fame.

Carter would make a different kind of baseball bat history four years later when he helped change the game by becoming the first player to use a maple bat in a major league game and the first to hit a home run with one.

Gonzo's broken-bat single, 2001

The spotlight can't burn any brighter, the pressure can't rise any higher. You approach the plate in the bottom of the ninth inning in the seventh game of the World Series with the game tied, the bases loaded, and perhaps the best closer in the history of baseball on the mound.

For Luis Gonzalez, who was mired in a dreadful slump in the postseason—hitting just .234 with only nine ribbies over three series—this was his scenario on Novermber 4, 2001. He faced off against Mariano Rivera with his trusty 34-inch, 33-ounce Rawlings 256B. Neither Rivera nor the bat would emerge unscathed.

Gonzalez had one factor in his favor. With only one out, the Yankees infield was drawn in, so the Arizona outfielder knew he didn't have to get much wood on the ball…and he didn't.

Rivera's cutter runs in on left-handed batters with such nasty movement that he breaks more bats than perhaps any other major league pitcher. His cutter did the job on Gonzo too, splintering the bat and producing a weak hit that under normal circumstances would have been an easy play for shortstop Derek Jeter.

With the infield in, however, nothing was normal. "I knew right when I hit it that it was going to drop," says Gonzalez, adding that the fractured lumber was "the last thing on my mind. I just wanted to touch first base."

Gonzalez was not particularly superstitious or attached to his bats, although he had certain routines—he always had the clubhouse guy add pine tar and rosin to his bats and brought his game bats out to the field with him at the beginning of warm-ups while most of his teammates waited until right before the game. In the case of the broken bat that won the Series, when he got it back afterwards he promptly and proudly donated it to the Hall of Fame. "I'm kind of a baseball historian, so I really loved the idea of having something to give back, to share with baseball fans."

The Big Papi show, 2004

When David Ortiz reached the majors in 1997, he used a 34-inch, 32-ounce Louisville Slugger C243 model made from traditional ash. He stuck with it throughout his days with the Minnesota Twins, but by the time he slugged his memorable game-winning home run for the Red Sox in Game 4 of the 2004 American League Championship Series, Ortiz's lumber had undergone several changes—one major, some minor.

The biggest change came in 2003, his first year in Boston. Just beyond midseason, he switched his bat preference to maple. Suddenly, Ortiz became a true slugger—he hit 20 of his 31 homers that year after placing his first maple order in late July. In 2004, he stuck with the maple but switched to a slightly longer bat, ordering two dozen 34½-inchers. Early in the season, he ordered 30 bats at that length but with a weight of 31½ ounces. The results? By season's end, he had punished American League pitching for 41 homers and 47 doubles. Then he hit .545 in the Division Series against the Angels, ending matters with a walk-off homer in the 10th inning of Game 3.

But Big Papi made his reputation as a great clutch hitter early on the morning of October 18, 2004, at Fenway Park, smashing a decisive 12th-inning homer in the fourth game off Yankees reliever Paul Quantrill after the Red Sox had lost the first three games of the ALCS. He took over again later the same day (the fifth game started only sixteen hours after the fourth game ended in the early hours of the day with Ortiz' walkoff homer), blasting another clutch homer in the eighth inning and delivering the game-deciding hit in the 14th. The Red Sox never looked back, winning Games 6 and 7 as well at Yankee Stadium and becoming the first team in baseball postseason history to overcome a three-games-to-none deficit. Four wins over St. Louis later, the Bosox had won their first World Series since 1918.

Chapter 4

SOME REAL CORKERS
And other sins with bats

> I'm going to get myself a corked bat and blast one out of here.
> What's the suspension for Old-Timers games, 10 years?
>
> *Vada Pinson, before a veterans' exhibition game*

Batters will try anything to gain an edge.

From the beginning, ballplayers have tampered with bats to improve their hitting. In the 19th century, Cap Anson was rumored to have plugged his bats with bamboo. (Bamboo is now used in composite bats that are legal in amateur ball.) But it was the birth of the long-ball era that gave impetus to the search for new tricks. In the 1923 season, Babe Ruth used a four-piece laminated bat designed by former Detroit star Sam Crawford, until American League president Ban Johnson banned it in August. (Laminated bats and multi-piece bats went in and out of the rule books, with the present rule—adopted in 1954—allowing only bats made out of a single piece of wood to be laminated.) Nine days after Johnson's ruling, St. Louis Browns slugger Ken Williams, who led the league in homers in 1922, had his bat confiscated by the Washington Senators, who protested that Williams had dug a hole in the wood and plugged it to make it lighter. Johnson benched that bat too.

In the 1920s, Browns hitting star George Sisler put Victrola phonograph needles into his bats; 30 years later, muscular Reds slugger Ted Kluszewski sank tenpenny nails into his oversized lumber to add extra weight, and diminutive White Sox second baseman Nellie Fox supposedly flattened his bats with a sledgehammer to widen the hitting surface (which also made bunting easier).

On opening day in 1932, Goose Goslin, then with the Browns, had his bat declared illegal, but not because of what was on the inside—Goslin came to the plate with a bat painted with a dozen black-and-white stripes running from the knob and widening by the barrel end. The bat's designer, Browns staffer Willis Johnson, called it "the War Club" (although the New York *Times* referred to it as the "prisoner's bat"), and he and Goslin hoped it would confuse and distract fielders. The umpires confiscated it immediately. Goslin argued that there was nothing in the rules prohibiting it, then gave up, grabbed another bat, and went 3-for-4 that day.

In a 1975 game, Bill Buckner's apparent go-ahead pinch single for the Dodgers became an out when Montreal catcher Gary Carter showed umpire Doug Harvey the deep grooves in Buckner's bat—a modification that supposedly makes a bat less likely to produce pop-ups. Buckner trotted out the all-purpose defense used by busted batters before and since: "I grabbed one of my practice bats by mistake."

Of course, the most common method of tampering with a bat is corking. Earl Weaver, a legendary talker, told this possibly tall tale on himself. When he played minor league ball at Class AA New Orleans in 1955, every Pelicans bat was corked—or so his story goes—and the 5-7, 160-pound Weaver cranked out six homers in one month. Then the umpires got wise. They raided the team's clubhouse, brought the bats onto the field, and destroyed the entire bunch.

Weaver hit no more homers that year and never reached the majors as a player. The Earl of Baltimore did, of course, reach the Hall of Fame as a manager, one known for being especially enamored of the three-run homer.

The corking process is quite simple. A player drills a hole 6 to 8 inches deep in the top of the barrel and then fills it with the contraband, adds some sawdust, sandpapers down the end of the bat, adds a little pine tar over the top and, voila, the bat is ready to go. (Some craftsmen actually use a wood burner to simulate the grain of the wood on the barrel's end.)

The logic behind cork is to make the bat lighter—usually by about an ounce-and-a-half, which increases bat speed and lets hitters wait on pitches a crucial split-second longer. This definitely improves the odds of making contact, but batters who claim that cork gives them extra pop need to brush up on their physics. With less mass at the point of contact, the bat can't drive the ball as far and cork actually turns home runs into long outs. Robert Adair, author of *The Physics of Baseball*, has argued that using shorter or lighter bats, or

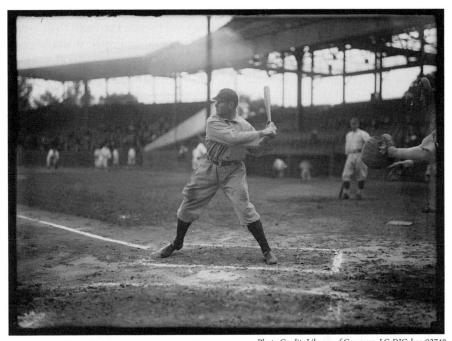

Photo Credit: Library of Congress, LC-DIG-hec-02748

In the 1920s, former Detroit Tiger star Sam Crawford, pictured here, designed a four-piece laminated bat that caught the attention of Babe Ruth, who began using it in games. American League President Ban Johnson then banned the use of the bat.

choking up, or even employing a cupped bat, would legally achieve the desired effect of increasing bat speed without sacrificing the density at the barrel.

Not everyone uses cork—alternate substances have even included a tube of mercury. Mercury is very heavy, but traditionally the tube is only partly filled, so the bat feels extremely light when held upright in the stance; as the bat whips through to the contact point, however, the mercury shifts and the bat becomes quite heavy.

One of baseball's most notorious incidents bypassed cork in favor of a product from the magical world of children's toys. In 1974 the New York Yankees were in a tight division race with Baltimore and Boston. On September 7 they lost the first game of a doubleheader to last-place Detroit; a defeat in the second game would drop New York into a tie with the Orioles and the Red Sox.

In the second inning of the nightcap at Shea Stadium (the club's two-year home while Yankee Stadium was being renovated), third baseman Graig Nettles smacked a homer to give New York a 1-0 lead. The next time up, Nettles rapped a single but his bat broke apart on contact and when it did six "super-balls" came bounding out. Home plate umpire Lou DiMuro called Nettles out for using an illegal bat. Yet nothing could be done to nullify Nettles' earlier blast—for one thing, no one could prove the same bat was used—and the home run stood up as the game's only run.

Nettles claimed that a fan in Chicago had given him the bat for good luck and that he'd picked it up by accident before heading to the plate. In the end, Nettles and his super balls couldn't save the Yankees, who still finished second behind Baltimore in the American League East.

More than 30 years after Nettles proclaimed his innocence, Tigers catcher Bill Freehan reflected on the goings-on, saying he knew plenty of guys who corked—teammate Norm Cash, for one—and that "every club had a wood-working shop." But the superballs trick was a new one—so creative, in fact, that everyone was taken by surprise. *Time* magazine cracked that "Nettles was the first man to bounce out to the third baseman, the shortstop, and the second baseman all at once."

In the aftermath of the incident, Major League Baseball implemented a rule calling for the suspension of players caught altering bats. Such a deterrent has not been enough to scare a lot of players away.

In the heat of the 1981 American League West race, for example, the Angels Dan Ford was kicked out of a game in Cleveland for using a corked bat and suspended for three additional games. It was particularly embarrassing for Ford, because earlier he had called corking allegations "garbage" when catchers Mike Heath of Oakland and Rick Dempsey of Baltimore accused the Indians outfielder of loading up a bat after he went on a surprising power display.

Houston's Billy Hatcher drew a 10-game suspension in 1987 for using a corked bat that had relief pitcher Dave Smith's name on it. Hatcher, who used the same model, acknowledged it was cheating but insisted it was purely accidental, saying he had mistakenly grabbed a bat that Astros pitchers corked for use in batting-practice home run derbies. "If I had known it was corked or whatever, I would have never gone up there to use it," said Hatcher. "I like to chop the ball down into the turf anyway."

Cincinnati's Chris Sabo was suspended seven games in 1996 for using a corked Mizuno R205 bat with Hal Morris' name on it, although Morris said he didn't use Mizuno bats and had donated that freebie bat to the pitching staff. Sabo also proclaimed his innocence—he said he simply grabbed a bat from a batboy after breaking one of his. "I have [only] three homers and 16 RBI [by late July], which is certainly no endorsement for the cork industry," Sabo remarked. Teammate Ed Taubensee ribbed Sabo, saying, "Let's see, Sabes popped to the shortstop with cork. Does that mean he would have popped to the pitcher without it?"

The next year in June, rookie Wilton Guerrero of the Los Angeles Dodgers raised his average from .246 to .292, then got busted on a groundout that resulted in an eight-game suspension. Not exactly your classic bat-corker—Guerrero was a 145-pound second baseman—he aroused the suspicion of umpires when he quickly turned from the basepath after making the out and hurriedly picked up pieces of his broken bat.

Of course, it's not always the crime that gets you in big trouble, sometimes it's the cover-up. This axiom became public knowledge during Watergate, but like many politicians since then the 1994 Cleveland Indians forgot their history lesson. In July in a game at Chicago, White Sox manager Gene Lamont got umpire Dave Phillips to confiscate the bat of surly slugger Albert Belle, arguing that it needed to be inspected for cork. While the bat was in the umpires' room, Indians pitcher Jason Grimsley hoisted himself into the duct space above the ceiling of the locker room and crawled along until he came to the room, where he swapped Belle's bat with one belonging to teammate Paul Sorrento. It was an escapade worthy of James Bond, but Grimsley didn't fool anyone and Belle was suspended for 10 days (later reduced to six days and seven games) for possession of a corked bat. Belle's teammates later said all of his bats were corked, which explains why Grimsley couldn't do the logical thing and replace the suspect lumber with another of Belle's bats. (In the 1995 playoffs, the Red Sox demanded that umpires check Belle's bat again. This time, it was pure wood.)

But while Belle was a feared slugger, he was also a known troublemaker. By contrast, Sammy Sosa had been a baseball hero, the home run hitter who, along with Mark McGwire, "saved" baseball after the disastrous players' strike of 1994-1995. But a few years later it all went sour for Sosa. It began with a decline in production, followed by an embarrassing scene in which he was caught on camera leaving the Cubs game early on the final day of the 2004 season. He was essentially run out of town by the media and fans because of that incident. Sosa's fall from grace was culminated by a disturbing appearance in 2005 in front of a congressional committee that left many fans believing he was part of the tainted steroid brigade. Looking back, however, his downfall's beginning can be traced to Slammin' Sammy's infamous corking escapade in 2003.

In June of 2003, the Chicago star was struggling with injuries and a slump—he was just 2-for-15 with one RBI and eight strikeouts after returning from a toe problem—when his bat shattered on a grounder in a home game against Tampa Bay. Umpire Tim McClelland found cork inside the bat and ejected Sosa, who drew an eight-game suspension (eventually reduced to seven). Although Sosa had a contract with the Easton company, he rarely used its bats, preferring Hoosier, Rawlings, and X Bats, 34½ inches and 32 ounces. The illegal bat was an X Bat, which had the handle shaved down, the finish removed, and a half-dollar-sized piece of cork inserted.

Instead of confessing, Sosa made matters worse for himself by offering only half an apology. He acknowledged ownership of the bat, explaining that he occasionally used it for batting practice and for home run exhibitions to entertain fans. "It is a mistake and I apologize to everyone, everyone who is embarrassed by this," he said. "I just picked the wrong bat heading to the plate." He was somewhat vindicated when MLB confiscated Sosa's 76 other game bats, all of which were cork-free, and the Hall of Fame checked the five Sosa bats in its possession and cleared all of them. Still, Sosa's image had its own crack in it, one from which he never really recovered.

One reason so many players cheat is that only a small percentage actually get caught. When Albert Belle was suspended, Chicago shortstop Ozzie Guillen said, "Believe me, he's not the only one corking his bat in the league. The main thing is he got caught."

Indeed, there have been plenty of players rumored to have packed their bats. In the 1980s, there were estimates that one in five hitters were on the cork. A few players even admitted it later.

Lenny Dykstra confessed that he corked his bat in the minor leagues, although he professed he never committed the crime in the majors. (Dykstra, who was also suspected of steroid use and who has since been arrested on embezzlement charges, is not necessarily seen as a paragon of truth.)

Lou Piniella said he corked his bat once—and only once—during his career, and that was against legendary spitballer Gaylord Perry. "I figured if he had an edge, I was going to have one, too," Piniella said. He blasted a homer off Perry but never used the bat again for fear of getting caught. "I was scared to take it out there again."

Norm Cash famously explained in *Sports Illustrated* how he doctored his bats. For those who credit Cash's 1961 season (41 homers, 132 RBI, and a league-leading .361 batting average for the Tigers) to his fortified bat, it should be noted that he used the corked bat in less-than-stellar seasons too.

Before the steroids era, accusations flew around certain teams—the Phillies and Royals of the 1970s and 1980s were rumored to have local carpenters do their dirty work. Players such as Hal McRae (Royals), John Mayberry (Royals and Blue Jays), Cecil Cooper (Brewers), and Doug DeCinces (Orioles, Angels) always faced suspicion, although they never were caught. McRae once had a half-dozen bats sawed in half by officials, but they were all clean.

Royals center fielder Amos Otis did confess after his playing days ended. "I had enough cork and 'superballs' in there to blow away anything," Otis said. "Over my whole career, it probably meant about 193 home runs for me." Otis finished with exactly 193 career home runs.

In 1987, Howard Johnson was corking his bat—at least that's what almost everyone outside New York thought. Entering the season, the Mets' third baseman had hit just 40 home runs in 1,185 career at-bats. But seeing everyday duty for the first time in his big-league career, Johnson suddenly started pounding the ball. By the end of July, he had 25 homers. Johnson attributed his power surge to consistent playing time (he had hit ten homers in just 220 at-bats the previous season); opponents said he was cheating.

The loudest whining emanated from Whitey Herzog and the Cardinals, then the Mets' archrivals. When Johnson, on successive nights at Busch Stadium in late July, beat St. Louis with a homer and sealed another victory with a second smash over the wall, Herzog went to work. After the second blast, the manager had catcher Tony Pena snatch the bat and hand it over to umpire crew chief Paul Runge. But Runge later returned the bat to Johnson, saying that "the grain looked like it had not been tampered with and the weight was right."

In the Mets' next series, at Montreal, Johnson again faced some questioning from the opposition. But the road trip ended with New York getting the last laugh. When the Mets left town, closer and league-leading prankster Roger McDowell—knowing the Cardinals were following them into Olympic Stadium—left one of Johnson's practice bats behind in the visiting clubhouse, with wine corks glued all over the outside. Herzog was not amused.

Soon thereafter, at Shea Stadium, the Cubs had Johnson's bat confiscated after homer No. 27. (Mets manager Davey Johnson tried retaliating by unsuccessfully asking that Chicago slugger Andre Dawson's bat also be taken out of action.) The next day, McDowell showed up in the clubhouse wearing a carpenter's belt that contained everything from cork to sandpaper to emery boards and even a saw.

Perhaps all the bat-checking rattled Johnson; or maybe he really was using cork (although league officials officially exonerated him). Or, the case could be made that Ho-Jo was simply bound to slow down sooner or later. Whatever the reason, Johnson hit only 11 home runs from July 31 to the end of the season. After his 36-homer output, he managed only 24 long balls in 1988. But Johnson bounced back with 36 homers in 1989 and hit an National League-leading 38 in 1991.

Not every corker is power hungry; some are simply aging players with slowing reflexes looking to get their bat around quicker as they chase whatever hits they still have left in their sticks. No player in baseball ever pursued his hits more rabidly, or more successfully, than Pete Rose. But a quarter-century after Rose passed Ty Cobb to become baseball's all-time hit king, evidence has surfaced that seemingly makes at least some small portion of that record ring hollow.

The first major public accusations came in 2001 when Tommy Gioiosa, a gambling pal of Rose who often placed bets for him, claimed in *Vanity Fair* that he'd personally done the corking on Rose's wood. A few years later an online gambling company, GoldenPalace.com, shelled out $103,631 to buy a Mizuno bat that belonged to Rose. The website's owner Drew Black boasted that this would prove Gioiosa's point. Golden Palace decreed that it would hold an event to saw the bat in half as a publicity stunt, and rumors even circulated that Rose would take part. But no one ever saw the sawing, and a year later the bat was quietly sold off again, reportedly for one-tenth the previous price. (There were rumors that Golden Palace had driven the initial price up by bidding against itself for publicity purposes. No one from the company would comment.) Rose denied everything at that time, but of course Rose also denied betting on baseball—and look how that turned out.

Photo Credit: Bill Schubert

But more credible, and thus more damning, was the bat revealed to the world in 2010 in an article on Deadspin.com.

It was one of Rose's thirty black PR4192 bats, weighing in at 31.6 ounces, 34 inches. He'd had Mizuno make this special model in 1985 as he closed in Cobb's record of 4,191 hits. After his career ended, Rose reportedly sold a chunk of his memorabilia off to pay some gambling debts. Among the bats bought by Steve Wolter—who had previously bought Rose's record-setting bat—was one that he eventually sold to a Pete Rose fan named Bill Schubert in exchange for cash and an autographed Babe Ruth ball from 1932.

Bill Schubert bought a bat used by Pete Rose because he'd been a fan of the Cincinnati legend. Then he discovered that the bat—and Rose—weren't exactly what they appeared to be.

The bat was authenticated as genuine. It had some unusual touches, like a heavier-than-usual taping on the handle and a white "14" painted on the head of the bat as well as the knob. Schubert started playing detective only after he saw a 1985 issue of a fledgling magazine called *Beckett Baseball Card Monthly* that had a cover photo of Rose in the on-deck circle with his bat. The picture had been shot over the July 4th weekend in Philadelphia, when the Reds' legend was a little over two months shy of the record. Schubert was struck by matching details like the scuff mark on the knob of the bat and three more along the handle. It seemed to match up perfectly with his bat. He contacted John Taube from PSA/DNA, one of the baseball memorabilia industry's leading authenticators. Taube agreed that Schubert's bat matched the one in the picture, meaning it had been used in that game.

After Schubert found an odd patch of wood on the bat head, a fellow collector encouraged Schubert to have the bat x-rayed. The results were definitive. The bat had clearly been hollowed out and filled with about six inches of some alternative material (whether it's cork is impossible to tell). Schubert now believes the white "14" was painted on the head as part of a cover-up, especially since other collectors (including Taube) had similar bats with what seems like drill holes underneath the number or X-rays showing cork inside.

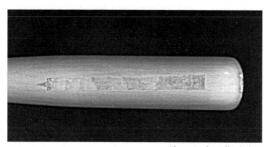

Photo Credit: Bill Schubert

After ascertaining that this Pete Rose bat was used in a game in 1985, Bill Schubert had it x-rayed. The image clearly showed that Rose had tampered with it.

Schubert says people in the industry told him the corking job was exceptionally well done—Rose apparently banged up the top of the bat to disguise the illegal work before painting the number on it. Not surprisingly, Schubert got negative press in Cincinnati and nasty emails from that area. He scoffs at their forced naiveté. "Come on, the guy lied to the whole country for twenty years and you take him at his word now?" he asks incredulously.

The Stockton, California, resident wasn't looking to cash in—he didn't sell the bat at the height of the hype. "I'll never have anything so unique again; it's a little piece of history that I unearthed because I did my homework." Instead of selling it, he bought a gun safe to protect it. Nor, he adds, was he looking to nail Charlie Hustle for this different type of hustle—he bought the bat innocently enough and remains a fan, saying, "This doesn't taint the record."

Instead, it reveals more nuances about Rose. "He was a cocky guy but it turns out he wasn't so confident," Schubert says. Rose knew he'd eventually reach Cobb's mark, but Schubert speculates that Rose didn't want to become the man with the most hits in baseball history while batting only .250. "He wanted to have a decent average when breaking the record," Schubert surmises. (This was not to be, however—the 44-year-old Rose was hitting .301 on June 9th but had fallen to .267 when he finally broke the record in September.)

Ultimately, Schubert says, we shouldn't be surprised that Rose cheated, given what we know about him, but he points out that it took "a lot of gall" for Rose to cork his bats when he was in the spotlight. The bat Schubert bought has a slight crack in the handle. "He was putting a lot at risk—what was he going to say if the bat had cracked open?"

These days Rose isn't saying much about it at all. Schubert saw Rose in Las Vegas and tried to talk to him but Rose had just two words for him: "Cork this."

In the baseball world, George Brett's reputation was the opposite of Rose's. Yet it was Brett who stood publicly accused of cheating in front a stadium full of fans. Of course, Brett's case didn't involve cork, but pine tar.

The legendary Pine Tar Incident stands out among all bat controversies for several reasons:

- The participants. The accused was George Brett, one of the game's greatest hitters and a future Hall of Famer, a player popular with the fans and the media; the accuser was Billy Martin, a volatile and vituperative genius with a penchant for sneaky and manipulative tactics. (Martin's previous foray into outrageous moves involving bats came when he was managing Oakland in 1982. The A's were playing a spring training game against the Padres in San Diego, and Martin was furious that he wasn't allowed to use a DH in the meaningless contest because the game was in an National League home park. To protest, Martin handed pitcher Steve McCatty a 15-inch toy bat, which he gamely took to home plate in his first at-bat. Umpire Jim Quick wasn't amused and refused to let McCatty swing the bat. McCatty took three called strikes with a real bat and sat down.)

- The teams. Anything involving the New York Yankees generates extra headlines, and the Kansas City Royals were the Yankees' biggest rivals from 1976 well into the '80s. The teams went head-to-head in the American League Championship Series four times in a five-year stretch.

- The material. Corking is cheating, for obvious reasons, but when a player puts pine tar on his bat to get a better grip, it isn't affecting the bat itself and is generally accepted throughout baseball.

On July 24, 1983, Brett, the Royals' third baseman, blasted a two-run homer off Yankees closer Goose Gossage with two out in the ninth inning at Yankee Stadium. The blow thrust Kansas City into a 5-4 lead. The Yankees were desperate for a win, having entered the game just two games out of first but trailing three other teams in the American League East. So Martin went to work. He somehow convinced crew chief Joe Brinkman and home-plate umpire Tim McClelland that the pine tar on Brett's bat exceeded the allowable 18-inch area and that this was such a heinous violation of the rules that the home run should not stand.

The umpires rescinded the homer, and Brett roared out of the dugout in furious protest—the image of Brett's face, contorted with rage while he was barely being restrained from a physical attack, remains the lingering visual reminder of the incident. But Brett was called out and the Yankees walked off the field with an apparent 4-3 victory.

As it turned out, though, the umpires had blown it. Brett was in violation of the rules, but their reaction was too severe. Rule 1.10 (b) said a pine-tar violation should prompt removal of the bat; there was no mention of the nullification of a hit. Rule 6.06 (d) permitted umpires to call batters out if they had altered bats "to improve the distance factor or cause an unusual reaction on the baseball." But pine tar, unlike cork or superballs, does not give the hitter any advantage. (In 1975, Houston's Jerry DaVanon had a single nullified in a similar incident, but that decision was also later deemed a mistake.)

Four days after the Royals-Yankees game, American League president Lee MacPhail overturned the umpires' decision. He targeted August 18 for

Photo Credit: National Baseball Hall of Fame

George Brett put a little too much pine tar on his bat. Billy Martin decided to make a big deal out if it. The rest is baseball history.

completing the suspended contest. New York owner George Steinbrenner and his Yankees argued MacPhail's recommended date and followed up with various legal moves and antics, but it was Yankee manager Martin's machinations that really turned the Pine-Tar Incident into a farce when August 18 rolled around.

First, Martin put pitcher Ron Guidry in center field and rookie lefthanded first baseman/outfielder Don Mattingly at second base as play in the suspended game was about to resume in the top of the ninth (since Brett's now-legal home run had given K.C. a one-run lead). The Royals were, of course, still at bat. Then, before new Yankees reliever George Frazier threw a pitch, Martin tried an appeal play, saying Brett failed to touch all the bases. Because the league used the closest regular umpiring crew rather than flying in the game's original umpires, Martin thought the ploy might work. But he had been outsmarted. MacPhail had obtained signed affidavits from the original umpires affirming that Brett hadn't missed a step.

After 12 minutes of action—Hal McRae struck out to end the top of the ninth and the Yankees were retired 1-2-3 in their half—the game was over, the Royals were 5-4 winners, and the Pine-Tar Incident was part of baseball legend.

Chapter 5

A DANGEROUS WEAPON
Flying bats and broken spears

I have observed that baseball is not unlike a war,
and when you come right down to it,
we batters are the heavy artillery.

Ty Cobb

For hundreds of years, people have thought of bats as dangerous, scary creatures, ducking away when any flew near.

Those nocturnal, flying mammals are actually a boon to mankind, of course, because they prefer eating mosquitoes to sucking human blood. But some bats—the wooden kind, to be precise—can be quite dangerous, especially when they wind up in the wrong hands.

Bob Ferguson had been a hitter—the game's first switch-hitter, in fact—but the former star of the Brooklyn Atlantics is remembered today, if he's remembered at all, for his nickname, Death to Flying Things, supposedly a tribute to his fielding skills.

But in the 1860s and 1870s, Ferguson was equally known for his sterling character. In an era when gamblers wielded heavy influence on the game and ballplayers were considered ruffians, Ferguson's integrity stood out. That's why he was elected president of the National Association of Professional Baseball Players in 1872, helping pave the way for the birth of the National League four years later. He also was called on to serve as an umpire even while an active player-manager.

In addition to his honesty, however, Ferguson had a hair-trigger temper. On July 24, 1873, he lost his cool and, with one unfortunate swing of the bat, a bit of the halo surrounding his reputation. Ferguson, still active with the Atlantics, was in Baltimore for a National Association meeting when he was called on to umpire a New York Mutuals-Baltimore Canaries game.

The Mutuals seized an 11-10 lead with a three-run rally in the ninth, but before the Canaries' half of the inning, an argument broke out between New York manager John Hatfield and his catcher, Nat Hicks, with each accusing the other of being in cahoots with gamblers. Ferguson, who had played with the Mutuals in 1871 before returning to the Atlantics, stepped in and, the Brooklyn *Eagle* reported, claimed Hicks was playing "as if he wanted the Mutuals to lose." When Hicks called Ferguson a "damn liar," the umpire snapped.

Ferguson grabbed a bat and swung at Hicks. He would have missed, but the catcher reflexively put up his arm and Ferguson made contact. According to the *Eagle*, the blow left Hicks with "an ugly wound." Other sources said it broke Hicks' arm in two places. (Hicks was knocked out of action for two months.) After the game, the crowd rushed Ferguson, who had to be escorted to the clubhouse by police. Hicks and Ferguson made up afterwards, but Ferguson was demoted to a back-up umpire the following season.

In modern times, the two most notorious incidents of violence with a bat featured pitchers in the villain role—for one, it was a rare stain on an otherwise sterling reputation, for the other, it seemed to solidify a nasty reputation in the minds of his opponents.

The crack of the bat is one of sports' most blissful sounds…except when it's cracking a skull instead of a ball. The sickening thud of Juan Marichal's bat connecting with Johnny Roseboro's head on August 22, 1965, at Candlestick Park in San Francisco in the middle of a tight pennant race between the two was, for decades, the lowest point in the generations-old rivalry between Marichal's Giants and Roseboro's Dodgers. (Unfortunately, in 2011 a new nadir was reached when a Giant fan was beaten senseless by Dodger fans at Dodger Stadium in L.A.)

Marichal, the Giants' ace, squared off against Los Angeles legend Sandy Koufax that day. It was the finale of a four-game series that had serious pennant implications. The two teams were already on edge—just two days earlier they'd nearly come to blows when the Giants accused speedy Maury Wills of purposely tipping Tom Haller's catcher's mitt with the bat trying for a free pass to first base; then Giant Matty Alou (Marichal's best friend) hit Roseboro's catcher's mask with his bat in retaliation and Roseboro threw the ball as close as possible to Alou's head on its way back to the mound. A fight was only nar-

Photo Credit: National Baseball Hall of Fame

Los Angeles catcher Johnny Roseboro needed 14 stitches to close up a two-inch gash after San Francisco pitcher Juan Marichal smashed him in the head with his bat.

rowly averted at that game.

But on August 22, Wills bunted for a hit, stole second, and scored his first time up. Marichal knocked him down on his next trip to the plate. Then he brushed back Ron Fairly. When Marichal came to bat in the third, Roseboro asked Koufax to retaliate. Koufax, however, refused to play headhunter, so Roseboro took matters into his own hands, firing a return throw to the pitcher so close that Marichal claimed it nicked his ear.

"Why did you do that," Marichal screamed at the catcher. A verbal exchange followed, but when Roseboro took off his mask and stood up, Marichal sensed an imminent attack and briefly but completely lost control. Using his bat as a bludgeon, Marichal smacked Roseboro three times on the head, giving him a concussion and sending blood streaming down his face from a deep two-inch gash that would require 14 stitches to close.

A full-throttle, 14-minute brawl erupted. Among the first on the scene was the Giants Willie Mays, who escorted Roseboro away, gently holding his opponent's head and crying, a scene shown on newscasts around the nation as much as the moment of Marichal's madness, which would also become a major spread in nearly every newspaper and many magazines in the country including *Life*.

Mays got Roseboro to the dugout where he couldn't get hurt further (and also couldn't launch a counterattack). But then Dodger Bob Miller charged Mays, Alou punched Miller, and Giant Tito Fuentes threatened to use his own bat on the Dodgers. Then Mays saw Dodger Lou Johnson about to jump an umpire; he tackled Johnson and got kicked in the head for his troubles. Mays would have to leave the game because of dizziness, but not before he slammed what would be the game-winning three-run homer off of Koufax in that inning, circling the bases with Roseboro's blood still on his shirt. It was his fourth homer in four games against L.A.

Marichal was fined $1,750 and suspended for eight days, with a behind-the-scenes order from league president Warren Giles that Marichal not pitch in Los Angeles in their next series, especially since the city was still reeling from the Watts riots. Mays received a rare standing ovation in Los Angeles, but for the Giants the damage was done—the suspension of Marichal may have cost them the pennant as they finished two games behind L.A. in the standings.

Roseboro sued Marichal for $110,000 over the incident, but they eventually settled out of court and later became good friends, spending time with each other's families. Roseboro admitted he had provoked the fight and lobbied for Marichal's admission to the Hall of Fame when it appeared that this incident might hurt his chances. Marichal publicly expressed remorse about using his bat as a weapon and later spoke at Roseboro's 2002 funeral (photos of the fight were featured in the program). "[His] forgiving me was one of the best things that happened in my life," said Marichal, who would also check in on Roseboro's wife Barbara for years afterwards. "I wish I could have had John Roseboro as my catcher."

There was no such reconciliation between Roger Clemens and Mike Piazza after two confrontations during the 2000 season. During interleague play, New York Yankee Clemens, who had a reputation as a headhunter, beaned the New York Mets' superstar catcher in the head and refused to apologize afterward. For baseball fans in New York, it upped the ante on the longtime crosstown rivalry. But things really exploded when the two teams met in the World Series that year, the first Subway Series in 44 years.

In the first inning of Game 2, Clemens fielded a two-out grounder and turned to throw—but the scenario was not that simple. First of all, Clemens had not caught the ball at all. He had picked up a chunk of wood that had splintered off Piazza's bat on a foul dribbler. Second, Clemens didn't throw toward first. Instead he threw the piece of wood at the Mets' catcher as he headed down the line.

Clemens claimed he reacted on instinct. He said that after thinking he had fielded the ball he realized it was the bat and was merely tossing it aside. Yet the media, numerous fans inside Yankee Stadium, and a huge national television audience sensed at least a malevolent spirit on the part of the Rocket, since it was coming from a player who was known for his short temper and confrontational attitude (and this was way before his steroid use had been publicly alleged).

Piazza kept his cool during the Series incident, snarling "What's your problem?" at Clemens but not charging the mound as the benches cleared. The hard-throwing veteran wound up pitching eight innings of two-hit, shutout ball that night. Trailing 6-0 in the eighth, the Mets rallied for five runs, including a two-run homer by Piazza, before falling just short. But after the game all anyone talked about was not Clemens' pitching nor Piazza's batting but Clemens' bat-throwing. (For instance, on the "The Daily Show with Jon Stewart," Stephen Colbert filed a report, still available on the show's website, with a bat fragment sticking out of his skull.) This incident remains the most memorable moment from that series and a definitive stain on Clemens' record.

Piazza may have exacted a measure of revenge in the 2004 All-Star Game when Clemens, then with the Houston Astros, was paired with Piazza as battery mates. The American League jumped all over Clemens, humiliating him with six runs in the first inning, and many people speculated that Piazza was tipping off the opponent batters, which seemed far-fetched to some but delicious to contemplate for anyone with a sense of justice.

Of course, hitters aren't always the innocent ones in these situations. In 1972, Oakland shortstop Bert Campaneris responded to a beanball with a beanbat. It was Game 2 of the 1972 American League Championship Series, and Campaneris, Oakland's catalyst, was 3-for-3 with two runs scored and two stolen bases when he came to bat in the seventh inning. Combative Tigers manager Billy Martin no doubt had seen enough of Campy—the A's were ahead in the game, 5-0—and it came as no great surprise when reliever Lerrin LaGrow threw at the Oakland speedster's legs. (Martin naturally denied any role in the incident.) LaGrow plunked Campaneris on the ankle. The 5'10", 160-pound Campaneris chose not to charge the 6'5", 220-pound reliever. Instead he impulsively hurled his bat at LaGrow's head. The pitcher hit the ground and escaped serious injury only by inches. Both benches emptied, led by Martin, who enjoyed a good brawl as much as anyone in baseball history. Umpire Larry Barnett restrained Martin; home-plate umpire Nestor Chylak held Campaneris back. After peace was restored, Chylak ejected Campaneris and LaGrow, later saying he removed the pitcher to avoid further conflict.

"The man's got no guts," Martin said of Campaneris. Urging a suspension, he declared, "There shouldn't be any place in baseball for anybody dumb enough to throw a bat."

Briefly, there wasn't: Campaneris was banned from the rest of the ALCS and fined $500, but commissioner Bowie Kuhn allowed him to play in the

Photo Credit: Library of Congress, LC-USZ62-119882 DLC

One of the ugliest racial attacks against Jackie Robinson came from the Philadelphia Phillies, who turned their bats on the rookie as if they were firing machine guns at him.

World Series, suspending him instead for the first seven games of the 1973 season. But in 1983, when Campaneris was on his last legs, he found a home in baseball in the most unlikely of places. The New York Yankees needed a backup infielder and so their manager gave the aging Campaneris the job. The manager? Billy Martin. Campaneris hit .322 in a part-time role in his final season in baseball.

The Ferguson, Marichal, Clemens, and Campaneris incidents, horrible as they were, all were crimes of passion, done in the heat of the moment. But one of the ugliest incidents in baseball history lacks that excuse, and it featured bats being used for violence, even if only as a metaphor.

The Philadelphia Phillies never laid a hand on Jackie Robinson; unlike some other opponents during Robinson's rookie season in 1947, they didn't bean him or spike him either. But with their mouths and with their bats, the Phillies made their feelings about integration perfectly clear. In a series that began one week after Robinson broke into the majors, they heaped three games' worth of hate on the Dodgers' rookie pioneer, spewing forth such venom as "they're waiting for you in the jungles, black boy"—and uglier taunts as well. Spurred on by their manager, a race-baiting Southerner named Ben Chapman, the Phils turned their bats on Robinson, reportedly pointing their handles at him as if the bats were machine guns and firing away.

Robinson, who had promised Branch Rickey he would turn the other cheek, nearly cracked. Yet he kept his cool and scored the lone run in the first game. His teammates rallied around him, coming to his support in a way that they might not have otherwise. Eddie Stanky challenged Chapman, "Why don't you guys go to work on somebody who can fight back? There isn't one of you [who] has the guts of a louse."

The white media and white fans, initially ambivalent to a large extent about the integration of baseball, also sided with Robinson. After commissioner Happy Chandler took Chapman to task, the Phillies manager was forced to pose for a publicity photo with Jackie. Neither Chapman nor Robinson was particularly happy about his role in baseball's equivalent of smoking a peace pipe, but they did it, standing together and holding…a bat.

Willard Brown actually had it worse than Robinson because it was his own teammates who turned on him. Brown was a great Negro Leagues slugger, but he got the short end of the stick when integration came to modern Major League Baseball. The Brooklyn Dodgers took great care to protect such players as Jackie Robinson, Roy Campanella, and Don Newcombe, and Cleveland Indians owner Bill Veeck did what he could to smooth the path for Larry Doby. The St. Louis Browns were far less sensitive. A dismal team with pitiful attendance, the Browns signed Brown and Henry Thompson on July 17, 1947, largely as a publicity gimmick to boost the gate.

Dubbed "Home Run Brown" by none other than Negro League slugging sensation Josh Gibson, Brown had smashed his way to stardom with long, heavy bats. He was told he didn't need to take any lumber to St. Louis because major leaguers got their pick of the litter. But when he showed up the Browns provided no bats for him. (Teammates also refused to throw with Brown or Thompson during warmups, isolating them as much as possible.) Stuck using pitchers' leftover 33-inch bats instead of his usual 36-inchers, Brown struggled in the majors. One day, he saw a 36-inch bat that teammate Jeff Heath had thrown away because part of the knob was broken off. Brown pulled it out of the trash, and on August 13 he took the bat to the plate at Sportsman's Park. That night, in the second game of a doubleheader, he smacked a two-run, inside-the-park homer off the center field wall, 426 feet from home plate. It was the first home run by a black player in American League history.

But when Brown returned to the dugout, he received the ultimate insult. Realizing it was his bat that had just made history, Heath was furious. In Brown's presence, Heath shattered the bat on the dugout wall. The statement was not subtle. Ten days later, Brown and Thompson were both released by St. Louis instead of being sent to the minor leagues for a chance to adjust. Thompson bounced back and had a career in the major leagues, but that was the only opportunity Brown received. He returned to stardom in the Negro Leagues, the Puerto Rican league, and later in the minor leagues. In a small measure of atonement, in 2006 he was elected to the Baseball Hall of Fame.

By 1954, integration was well under way and Jackie Robinson was acknowledged as one of the game's greatest players. Robinson's promise to hold his temper in check for three seasons was a thing of the past. So Robinson found himself ensnared in another bat controversy on a rainy night in Milwaukee, when he got ejected for arguing with the umpire. Frustrated, he tossed his bat toward the dugout. The wet stick slipped out of his hands, skimmed the dugout roof, and slid into the stands.

Initially, it appeared the bat had brushed against an usher's cap, and Robinson used body language to indicate it was an accident and that he was sorry. But Braves fans yelled nasty threats, prompting the police to provide protection for Robinson when the game was called after five innings.

The next day, a lawyer came forward claiming that Mrs. Peter Wolinsky had a "nice bump" on her head and might file suit. Robinson called her and apologized. By the second day, the lawyer declared that both Wolinskys, the husband and wife, had been bonked and suffered concussions. He promised a lawsuit unless baseball punished the troublemaker. The Dodgers moved on to

Chicago, where Robinson was the object of heavy booing. Early the following week, a third person claimed injury from the flying bat. But the commissioner's office soon handed down a complete "not guilty" verdict, refusing to punish Robinson beyond a $50 fine for continuing his argument with the umpire from one inning to the next before being tossed in the game in Milwaukee. The jeering, however, did not let up as opposing fans stepped up the heckling. Robinson eventually wrote an article in *Look* magazine ("Now I Know Why They Boo Me") part of which told his version of these events.

Ted Williams had a fiery intensity that could nearly match Robinson's and had an equally tempestuous relationship with the fans that helped cause problems for him when he accidentally flung a bat into the stands.

Williams had stunned the baseball world in 1957 by hitting .388 at age 39. In 1958 Williams had a second straight batting crown in his sights when he hit a September slump soon after his 40th birthday. Nobody took hitting more seriously and more personally than Williams, and his frustration spiked on September 21 when he took a called third strike in a game against Washington at Fenway Park.

Williams tried to fling the bat to the ground in disgust, but he had so much stickum on his hands that the bat stuck to him as he swung his arms down and it didn't come loose until he flung them upward. Then the bat soared into the stands, where it struck a fan in the head—and not just any fan, but 60-year-old Gladys Heffernan, the housekeeper for Red Sox general manager Joe Cronin. (Heffernan was sitting in her boss'—and Williams' boss'—box seat.)

The temperamental superstar immediately ran over and apologized to Heffernan, who was bleeding from the head but not seriously injured. When Williams cried while visiting her in the first-aid room, Heffernan told him she knew it was an accident. Still, the Fenway crowd booed the bat-flinging, and the episode became national news when the story and photos went out over the wires. Williams, who had been fined earlier in the year for spitting at fans, was docked only the standard $50 for bat-throwing after the league office declared his actions were unintentional. Some in the press came to Ted's defense—*New York Times* columnist Arthur Daley wrote of Williams' "agonizing remorse" and how he was "whipped by an inner punishment" after the incident.

On the field, however, Williams quickly rediscovered his stroke, going on an offensive tear and winning his sixth and last batting title with a .328 average. For Christmas that year, Williams sent Heffernan a diamond watch.

As scary as it must be to have a bat come flying at you in the stands, at least fans at field level are expected to be alert. No one expects a player to get hurt by a bat flying out of the stands...especially if he literally asked for it. Reliever Akinori Otsuka, a veteran Japanese pitcher, signed with the San Diego Padres and was on his way to a standout rookie season in 2004 when he was asked by a fan to autograph a bat. Sure, Otsuka said and motioned to the fan to throw it on down. Big mistake. It seems another fan thought Otsuka was signaling to him, so he simultaneously tossed Otsuka a ball and a piece of paper. Perhaps with the "keep your eye on the ball" mantra drilled into him once too often, Otsuka tried to catch the ball and paper and glanced away from the bat, which bonked him in the head. Fortunately, the righthander wasn't seriously injured, although he was bruised. Afterward, Padres manager Bruce Bochy, a former catcher, offered some of the sagest advice he'd ever uttered to a pitcher: "Next time, catch the bat and let the paper hit you."

Baseball's worst tragedy involving bats transpired entirely off the field, and the bats never were used in a game. In 2008 former San Francisco Giants prospect John Odom tried latching on with the Calgary Vipers in the independent North American Baseball League. But a conviction for assault during his teens meant Odom couldn't cross the border, so Calgary looked to trade him. The Laredo Broncos of the independent United League offered a hitter for Odom, but that deal didn't work out. Then they offered $1,000 for the contract, but the Vipers refused because of concerns it might make the franchise look shaky financially. So the Broncos came up with way around that—they offered ten bats—34-inch long C243 model black bats from Prairie Sticks—worth about $665.

With little leverage to make a trade, the Vipers took the deal, but when the media started joking about it the Broncos and Vipers tried reassuring Odom that there was no insult intended. At first, Odom gave interviews and seemed cheerful about the whole experience, even embracing the "Batman" nickname. But soon he became depressed and began unraveling on the mound and in the clubhouse. Before the season was out he had quit, saying he needed time away from the game. Six months after the trade, Odom, who had struggled with drugs in his younger days, was dead at 26; the official ruling was an accidental overdose of heroin, methamphetamine, alcohol, and benzylpiperazine. The bats themselves were originally intended to be auctioned off by the Vipers for charity, but Ripley's Believe It Or Not offered $10,000 as a donation to the club's children's charity and took the bats to put on display at one of their exhibits to celebrate one of baseball's oddest trades. However, since Odom's death the company has put the bats away. A recent search of the Ripley's website revealed no mention of them.

Chapter 6

EVOLUTION OF A WOODEN STICK
Changes in shape and size

> They give you a round bat
> and they throw you a round ball
> and they tell you to hit it square.

> *Willie Stargell*
> *(Also attributed to Hank Sauer, Pete Rose, Ted Williams, others.)*

The earliest baseball bats were primitive clubs.

They were often flat, and most were handmade from a variety of wood. Some were carved from tree limbs, some reconfigured from ax handles. The game evolved, however, and by the mid-1850s bats had become rounded (except for a specialized flat bunting bat). By that point, many of the better players also were having professional wood-makers carve their bats. In the early years, nearly every kind of wood—sycamore, cherry, spruce, chestnut, poplar, and basswood—was used, depending on what players could get their hands on. For a brief run, willow was the popular choice.

The first bat-related rules were drawn up in 1859 when the Professional National Association of Baseball Players Governing Committee decreed that bats could not be more than 2½ inches in diameter. (That was expanded to 2¾ in 1895.) In 1869 the year professional baseball was born with the Cincinnati Red Stockings, lumber was limited to 42 inches in length. (The rule is irrelevant in modern baseball, because no one today could handle a stick that long. Back in the days of underhand pitching, no curveballs allowed, and batters looking for balls in a specific zone, hitting was a very different art.)

The earliest bats were nearly as fat at the handle as they were at the barrel, although they gradually began slimming down near the grip area. In the 1860s, players also began wrapping twine or cord around the handle to improve their grip. The most significant development was the birth of the knob, which helped players control their swing. Still, the game itself was very much in flux, and from 1885 through 1893 players were again allowed to use bats flattened on one side. Though few players liked hitting with them, they did become popular for bunting (even though bringing a flat bat to the plate was a dead giveaway). Finally flat bats, bats of soft wood (often used for bunting too), and bats that were sawed off at the end were disallowed for good.

By the 1870s and 1880s ash and hickory had emerged as the most popular woods. Albert Spalding was a talented major leaguer who was also a savvy innovator and entrepreneur. He began churning out cheap bats in 1879 and was among those who figured that as horse-drawn carriages were being phased out in the new age of automation, the spokes or "tongues" from wagon wheels could easily be recycled into bats. Back then, manufacturers solicited wood from the general public for bat-making—an ad for Spalding's Wagon Tongue Black Tipped Bats informed the public that "a liberal price will be paid for straight grained, well seasoned, second growth Ash Sticks."

Meanwhile, throughout the dead-ball era, players largely stuck with those thick-handled bats. In the early 20th century, Ty Cobb used a bat that was 34½ inches long and weighed 40 ounces. Players like Cobb and Honus Wagner, who used 35-inch bats weighing up to 38 ounces, spread their hands several inches apart to enable them to control these behemoths and slap at the ball.

The game changed radically in 1920 with the emergence of Babe Ruth, the banishment of the spitter, and the use of more new baseballs per game. Hitters suddenly "dug the long ball," yet they didn't forswear the heavy sticks of their forebears. Ruth copied the great Joe Jackson and often used hickory, a much heavier and more durable wood that was in vogue throughout the dead-ball era. The Bambino's bats were, not surprisingly, massive—he used 36-inch bats his first few years as an outfielder, then dropped to 35 inches around 1925. His early bats tipped the scales at anything from 40 to 51 ounces, although Ruth claimed to have even used 54-ounce clubs. (He mostly used the heaviest ones only in spring training.) Starting in 1926 he lightened up a bit, ordering some 36-ouncers although most were still in the 38-42 ounce range. It wasn't until 1929, on the downside of his storied career, that the Babe began using bats weighing a "flimsy" 35 ounces. "My idea on weight is that you should use a bat as heavy as you can handle," Ruth wrote after his playing days. "If you can

Photo Credit: *National Baseball Hall of Fame*

Ty Cobb, like other great hitters of the deadball era, used an enormously heavy bat—his was 40 ounces—but spread his hands apart so he could slap at the ball.

swing a bat weighing, say, 38 ounces as fast as one weighing 35 ounces, you're bound to get a longer hit. What's more, you get real solid timber in the heavier bats, and that, too, adds to driving power."

Still, there was one pronounced change in this era. It came from Rogers Hornsby, a man who took his job so seriously he wouldn't read or go to movies for fear of straining his "hitter's eyes." He also was so confident that he proclaimed, "I don't like to sound egotistical, but every time I stepped up to the plate with a bat in my hands I felt sorry for the pitcher." Hornsby emerged as a superstar right at the end of the dead-ball era, then made a remarkable transition in Ruthian times. After hitting 36 home runs overall in his first five full seasons, Hornsby responded to the changing game by cranking 21 in 1921 (while also leading the National League in average, hits, doubles, triples, runs, and RBI) and then leading the league in homers with 42 in 1922 (while also finishing on top with a .401 batting average).

Hornsby has been remembered and revered for his hitting prowess, but few recall that he also helped transform the bat itself, starting the trend toward tapered handles. He realized that the thinner bottom would help him get the bat head through the zone more quickly. Although some lesser lights used tapered bats before Hornsby was even in the majors, he was the one who drew attention to the tactic and thus is credited as the first player to use a genuinely tapered bat. Even Ruth, whose weighty bat was decidedly old-fashioned soon saw the wisdom of Hornsby's modern ways. But not surprisingly, given his personality, the Sultan of Swat took it to an extreme—his bats had a huge barrel then narrowed more sharply than the Rajah's. And as Ruth went at that time, so went baseball. The trend toward tapered handles had begun in earnest.

In recent years, of course, scientists have proven that Ruth and his contemporaries may have hampered their long-ball hitting with their heavy bats. Physics experiments have demonstrated that bat speed matters in creating power and that it is easier to generate more speed with a lighter bat. Players had gradually been figuring that out on their own, despite most of them not having college degrees and without actually contemplating the laws of physics. By the 1930s the heaviest bats shrunk to 35 or 34 ounces, and then such players as Ted Williams and Stan Musial brought it down to 33 and lower. By

Photo Credit: Library of Congress, LC-USZ62-71763

While Babe Ruth relied on mammoth weapons to club his home runs, he did follow Rogers Hornsby's lead and taper the handle, creating a trend throughout baseball. (Insert shows Ruth in clubhouse after game.)

the 1950s Hank Aaron was often using a 32-ounce bat—and he managed to hit a fair number of home runs in his career. (Heavy bats enjoyed a short-lived comeback among some sluggers in the 1960s when Orlanda Cepeda and Dick Allen broke the 40-ounce barrier and Roberto Clemente weighed in with a 39-ouncer.) The desire for lighter bats meant the end of hickory, a hard and strong wood that produced heavier bats. Ash, always popular, became the industry standard. As the bats got lighter, they often got shorter—bats typically had been 35 inches or more, but by 1949 more than one-fourth of Louisville Slugger's major league clients used 34 or 34½-inch bats, and by 1959 that number had climbed to nearly 40 percent.

The push for lighter bats remained relentless, and by the 1970s players had found a new way to achieve their goal: cupping. The Hanna Manufacturing Company, a tool and farm implement business that had begun making bats in the 1920s, was the first company to make a "cupped" bat in which the end is carved out, making the bat ½-ounce to a full ounce lighter and shifting its center of balance farther down the barrel. This process started in the early 1940s, but the cupped bats never caught on in Major League Baseball. Cupped bats did, however, find their way to Japan, where they became commonplace. In 1970, George Altman, a former major leaguer playing in Japan, gave one of

The quest for ever lighter bats eventually led to the C271 Louisville Slugger—the model that outfielder Jose Cardenal used to introduce the cupped bats to the major leagues.

those bats to St. Louis outfielder Jose Cardenal. Cardenal was initially impressed by the hard, durable yellow wood (which he thinks may have been bamboo) and bought a dozen from a Japanese company. The company also explained to him the benefits of cupping. The bats attracted protests from opposing teams, Cardenal recalled, but he kept using them and finally the commissioner's office declared them legal. (The cupped end can be carved no deeper than one inch and no wider than two inches in diameter.)

Cardenal then was offered a contract by Louisville Slugger, which said it could replicate the cupped end. (Ironically, Hanna went out of business just a few years later.) The bat that Louisville Slugger created was called the C271 model (because Cardenal was the 271st player whose name started with a "C" to have a bat model named for him) and has become one of the most popular models of all-time. Ken Griffey, Jr., and Albert Pujols are among those who have toted Cardenal's model to the plate. Today, nearly one-third of all players swing cupped bats. The handle is not overly thin and the barrel is not too heavy. "It's just a very well-balanced bat," Cardenal said. "You put it in your hands and you can feel it."

In modern times, better training methods and the increased usage of relief pitchers have yielded fastballs thrown harder on average than ever before. Meanwhile, pitchers have also begun mixing in more cutters and splitters with such late-breaking movement that hitters need to let the ball travel as deep into the zone as possible before whipping the bat quickly around to the point of impact. Even cupping wasn't enough for some players. For example, Tony Gwynn used 30-ounce or 31-ounce bats, and players now rarely go above 32 or 32½ ounces. In the never-ending pursuit of whip-like bats, players who grew up with aluminum bats have pursued even skinnier handles—ones that remind them of the fat-barreled, thin-handled bats they used to crush the ball in the amateur ranks.

Eventually, however, the quest for lighter bats and skinnier handles would—in tandem with the introduction of a new wood—create increased problems…in addition to increased run production.

Chapter 7

EXPLODING BATS
Changes in density and material

> When you first use them,
> it's a totally different feel from a normal bat.
> I mean, totally different.
> After you use them, you don't want to go back.
>
> *Toronto slugger Joe Carter,*
> *the first player to use a maple bat in the majors,*
> *on his conversion from ash to maple*

The light and thin-handled bats helped stoke the power surge of the 1990s, but like other "advances" that helped fuel the growth in home run hitting, there was a price to be paid. Bats began shattering in record numbers. "When they're wanting the huge barrel, real thin handle…the bat's going to explode," said Louisville Slugger player liaison Chuck Schupp, who says Paul O'Neill and Jeff Bagwell were perhaps the last players to use a balanced bat—34 inches and 34 ounces for O'Neill and 33 each for Bagwell—which, says Schupp, is the key to a longer-lasting bat.

The home runs mashed in the steroid era also forced pitchers to throw inside—hit-by-pitcher numbers jumped in the mid-1990s and didn't decline again until 2006—and the willingness to pitch inside, plus the popularity of the cutter thrown by Mariano Rivera and other mere mortals who copied him, made those slim-handled sticks even more vulnerable to snapping.

Major league teams began ordering about twice as many bats as they did in the 1980s. Several bat manufacturers have said players would get more durability and pop with heavier, more balanced bats. But it wasn't only the shape and size of the bat that was evolving; it was the wood itself that changed. In the 1990s, maple bats started creeping into the starting lineup, and that wood's popularity exploded after Barry Bonds hit 73 home runs using exclu-

Maple bats started being produced by boutique companies but quickly grew so popular that even the famed Louisville Slugger is now made from maple as often as it is from the traditional ash.

sively maple bats in 2001. Many players credited maple with increasing their home run totals, but some critics said it was not just the wood's popularity that was exploding—it was the bats themselves.

Maple is a harder, denser wood than ash, which has convinced many ballplayers that it gives them more pop. This is not scientifically true—Major League Baseball commissioned a maple-versus-ash study at the Baseball Research Center at the University of Massachusetts-Lowell. The study used a potato gun to fire balls and 34-inch, 32-ounce bats of an identical model, the C271, made of either ash or maple. The result? A Louisville Slugger ash bat produced a slightly higher exit velocity than the maple models. But ballplayers believe what they want to believe when it comes to bats. As a result, these days, even Louisville Slugger makes half its bats out of maple.

Maple is denser than ash, which does allow players to use smaller bats and have the same overall weight. But the closed-grain wood also has less flexibility and a smaller sweet spot than ash bats. Maple bats are harder to make with consistency because of the wood's high moisture content. In fact using maple wasn't even feasible until new technology in the form of vacuum and radiation kilns came along in the 1990s. While traditional kilns reduced the moisture level to about 15 percent, the newer models could get it down to less than half that. That put maple wood in play.

Since maple is more solid, it doesn't flake the way ash does and there-by gives the impression of being more durable. Early maple users like Cliff Floyd who did not choose super-skinny handles found themselves produc-ing bloop singles with maple bats instead of broken-bat outs with ash. But because maple is heavier and players want lighter lumber, many chose even thinner handles, causing even more broken bats. (The ideal moisture content for maple would be 10-12 percent but that would make most bats too heavy and therefore maple would not be commercially viable.)

The truth is, however, that these maple bats are breaking in a way that has become dangerous. Since maple doesn't have the grains of ash and flaking isn't a problem, it's difficult to detect hairline fractures in a maple bat. So play-ers are more likely to be swinging a bat that should have been retired. With a closed-grain wood and without ash's flexibility, maple bats don't splinter—they snap, sometimes sharply, into two or more pieces.

"When maple breaks, it flies apart, that's just the characteristic of the wood," says Jim Wells, who spent a career in the hardwood lumber industry before becoming a co-founder of Mattingly Sports, which began making bats in 2005.

With the influx of skinny-handled bats made of maple, someone was bound to get hurt. The first someone was Rick Helling. Helling, a former 20-game winner in the majors, already had rebounded from one bad come-backer—in the spring of 2004 the right-hander was contending for a spot in Minnesota's rotation when a line drive broke his leg. In 2005, Helling was at-tempting a comeback with Milwaukee's Class AAA Nashville affiliate when he was battered by a bat instead of a ball.

Hitting against Helling, New Orleans' Craig Kuzmic fouled off a pitch, breaking his bat in the process. Unfortunately, Kuzmic's bat shattered and a 15-inch sliver rocketed to the mound, where Helling unsuccessfully tried to jump out of the way. The chunk of wood impaled Helling in the left forearm, going more than three inches deep. Catcher Julio Mosquera nearly fainted when he saw the bat protruding from his battery mate. Helling said he was not in tremendous pain at that point. The pain came later, after the Nashville trainer covered the pitcher's arm with a towel and led him into the clubhouse. There the team doctor had to tug to remove the wood."When they took it out, that was really painful," Helling said, adding that he had "never heard of anything like this in baseball."

Helling was taken to Vanderbilt University Medical Center for x-rays and cleansing; he needed seven stitches to close the wound. Helling (who got the win that night) was nearly hit by two more broken bats (also maple) in his next start. Two months after his frightful moment, Helling was called up by the Brewers, for whom he pitched in relative safety.

Also in 2005 San Diego pitcher Clay Hensley took a shot to the head from a fragment of maple and needed four stitches. The following year there were three instances in a month—twice barrels broke off and flew into the stands, though no one was hurt; Arizona's Eric Byrnes slammed a maple bat in frustration after a pop-up and it exploded, with shards wounding Florida catcher Miguel Olivo in three places. In 2007 a New York Mets fan named Jim Falzon suffered severe and disfiguring facial injuries at Shea Stadium on a broken bat fly ball by Luis Castillo, using a Rawlings maple bat belonging to teammate Ramon Castro.

Major League Baseball raised the maple bat issue in the collective-bargaining negotiations. The union not only opposed a ban but wasn't even open to the idea of new specifications for maple bats. Then in 2008 the issue became impossible to ignore.

On April 16 Pittsburgh Pirate Nate McClouth smacked a pitch down the right field line. In the dugout, hitting coach Don Long was watching the ball and so he didn't realize that his life was in danger—a huge segment of jagged maple was flying at his head. As McLouth raced to second with a double, Long was slammed in the face just below the eye by the remains of his bat, which sliced his cheek muscle and damaged the nerve underneath before lodging under his skin. Long saw the blood puddling on his shoes then he was taken to the clubhouse for help. Eventually a doctor removed the wood and sewed his face back up with ten stitches.

In the aftermath, MLB again reached out to the union about the issue. Nine days later, both sides received another jolt. Colorado's Todd Helton's maple bat shattered at Dodger Stadium and this one injured a fan, a woman named Susan Rhodes, who wound up with a shattered jaw that required surgery utilizing screws and a titanium plate to hold her jaw together. Two months after that incident, MLB's Safety and Health Advisory committee met to begin discussing maple bat regulations; on that very day, home plate umpire Brian O'Nora had to leave a game in Kansas City when a shard of maple sliced his forehead open after Olivo's bat broke on a ground out. Punctuating the season was a new and unofficial record set in September by Oakland rookie Cliff Pennington, who managed to break three bats on foul balls in the course of a single plate appearance.

Sam Holman, of the pioneering Sam Bats used by Bonds and others, was among those who spoke out saying that many bat companies had rushed to cash in on the maple bat craze and had cranked out sub-par products, using either inferior wood or improper drying techniques or both. Others have said companies created brittle bats by drying them to 5% moisture content to make production more commercially viable. "There were smaller companies using furniture grade material (which is very weak)," says Carolina Clubs founder Kevin Lane.

"Bat manufacturers are some of the least knowledgeable about wood that I've met," says Jim Wells, who says that it is not just drying them too much but also too quickly that can cause honeycombing in the wood and weaken the bat.

It is not just the maple *per se* but the combination of maple bats and big barrels with skinny handles that is threatening to become lethal—McLouth's bat was 33½ inches and only 30 ounces, which meant it had a disproportionately skinny handle. (Sam Holman at one point shrunk the barrel on his maple bats to increase balance and improve aerodynamics.) Jim Anderson, founder of MaxBats, says players shouldn't swing anything with a weight to length differential greater than -2, meaning a 33-inch bat should weigh no less than 31 ounces.

Of course, ash bats can splinter too. In one of the worst cases, back in 1976 Los Angeles Dodger Steve Yeager nearly got killed. As a catcher Yeager was accustomed to getting banged up: There were pitches in the dirt, foul tips and collisions at the plate, along with the wear and tear of squatting in heavy equipment in hot weather for hours each day. Yet in the on-deck circle most players let down their guard. On September 6 in San Diego, Yeager was awaiting his turn to bat when Bill Russell broke his bat on a pitch; a large chunk of wood flew back and lodged in Yeager's throat, opening a wound that required nine stitches. The doctors told Yeager that an inch to the right and the splintered bat would have severed an artery, possibly killing him. (Soon thereafter, Yeager devised a flap that could be attached to the bottom of the catcher's mask, shielding the exposed area of the neck. Of course, that would not have helped him in the on-deck circle, where there was no protection.) And in 1993 the Angels Tim Salmon was stabbed in the triceps while waiting on deck after Stan Javier's bat shattered.

Photo Credit: MLB

Alarmed by the number of flying bat shards and the injuries that resulted, Major League Baseball took action in 2008 with a study that revealed that maple bats are indeed more likely to break violently than ash bats.

But after the 2008 season, Major League Baseball was concerned enough about the differences between maple and ash that the commissioner did what any good seamhead would do—look at the statistics. A study found that from July through September 2008 there were 2,232 bats broken during games, 756 of which broke into multiple pieces. Maple bats were three times more likely than ash to break into multiple pieces, largely a result of low "slope of grain" (jargon for how straight the grain is) or ruptures in the wood. Maple was four times more likely than ash to break over slope-of-grain problems.

In 2009 the independent Frontier League banned all maple bats. For the majors and affiliated minor leagues, MLB implemented new grading requirements for the bats' slope of grain, stricter tracking requirements for each manufacturer's bats, and several other rules. Players whose bats broke in two more than ten times a year would have to sit through a consultation meeting with bat experts from the MLB and union offices. (An MLB spokesman would not name names but says that several did and some switched bats after their enforced education.)

In 2009 the rate of breakage dropped by a third, and by 2010 the rate was half that of 2008. Tighter restrictions were added for new players, including a smaller maximum barrel of 2.61 inches (though most players didn't use the maximum 2¾ inch barrel anyway) and a bigger minimum for handle size.

Michel Laplante, founder of B45 bats, says the regulations were good because it drove up the prices for those who were trying to get away with inferior grains, which leveled the playing field for those striving to provide the best wood. Max Bats' Jim Anderson objected to the extra regulations at first but now supports them, saying, "It has been a really great way to keep as many bad bats out of the game as possible."

Still, Anderson says enforcement could be tighter and that the maximum barrel size could be reduced to 2½ inches. And danger remains. In 2010 rookie Tyler Colvin, while scoring from third, was impaled in the chest by a piece of a broken maple bat belonging to teammate Wellington Castillo. Colvin was taken to the hospital where a tube was put in his chest to prevent a collapsed lung. And in 2011 a fan in Kansas City was hospitalized and needed surgery after the Angels Torii Hunter's maple bat snapped and a chunk smashed into her head.

MLB could push the regulations further to make handles thicker, though some maple makers oppose that notion, worrying that thick-handled bats would make maple so heavy players would switch away. Maple remains popular enough that some companies began looking for new maple sources in places like Russia and China. "Siberian maple grows slower because it is colder there and that makes a denser bat," says Don Fine, owner of Viper Bats and other companies. But the costs are prohibitive and he hasn't been able to get enough wood to really test the bat's mettle against live pitching.

Roland Hernandez, a former research engineer for the USDA Forest Service and the founder of Rock Bats of Monona, Wisconsin, focuses on the safety of maple bats by promoting straight-grain over slope-of-grain. On his website, www.rockbats.com, Hernandez uses the dot of ink now required on all maple and birch bats by major and minor league baseball (as an indicator of the quality of the grain) to demonstrate the differences in the angles of grain on different handles. Hernandez then shows what happens when both types of grains break—the straight-grained bat will rupture but stay together, rather than explode into multiple pieces.

While the spotlight has been on maple in recent years, ash is facing a crisis as well, one that potentially has more devastating long-term consequences. Weakening the ash bats is not a skinny handle or a poor slope of grain but a tiny metallic green beetle, the Emerald Ash Borer. The borer, an invasive species from Asia first discovered in the United States in Michigan in 2002, probably arrived in wood packing materials. The beetle destroys ash trees, including the northern white ash used for bats. In less than a decade it has found its way into 14 states and two Canadian provinces, destroying tens of millions of trees. Since forests in New York and Pennsylvania have both been victimized (though not the ones where Louisville Slugger gets its trees) there is serious concern about the long-term viability of the northern white ash. In addition to the Emerald Ash Borer beetle crisis, there is some concern that the flourishing deer population, which eats the young trees, is taking its toll on the ash, making it harder to find good wood. (The bats are made from the lower part of the tree because there are too many defects in the wood from the upper sections of the tree.)

Although the borer has not yet impacted bat production, by 2011 fears were so high that Louisville Slugger partnered with The Nature Conservancy on a "Don't Move Firewood" campaign, since transported wood seems to be the most common way the beetle travels from one forest to another. The company is also partnering with various government agencies, including the U.S. Department of Agriculture, which has a website, www.stopthebeetle.info, for anyone who spots a borer. "There is a sense of panic," says Carolina Clubs owner Kevin Lane, explaining that logs can now only be taken from a 50-mile radius and not hauled over long distances in New York.

Even before the spread of the borer intensified, companies were always searching for other sources of top-notch wood, but no other wood has yet

The best new hope for an alternate wood source appears to be yellow birch. Manufacturers and hitters alike praise the fact that it is strong like maple but flexible like ash.

connected for hitters in the same way as ash and maple. A small company in Pennsylvania called BWP Bats has been making red oak bats, which it says blends some of the best qualities of ash and maple bats. But red oak has yet to catch on, in large part because it has a lot of knots and other flaws. BWP is an offshoot of Brookline Wood Products, a decades-old company that makes furniture squares and hardwood floors, so it can afford to experiment with making red oak bats because the unused wood will find a second life as furniture; BWP also saves on trucking costs because it takes all its ash, maple, and red oak from within 75 miles of its mill.

Hillerich & Bradsby, the makers of the Louisville Slugger, thought it had found a solution that provided the best of both worlds: European beech. Those trees provide bats that are heavier and more flake-resistant than ash but lighter and more flexible than maple—plus they yield a more productive harvest and break less frequently in the lathing process than maple. (Many American beech woods have been infested with beetles, and some lack the European variety's strength.) David Ortiz and Adam Dunn were among those on the front line of these lumber wars, armed with wood nurtured in a mysterious forest in the Old World. Louisville Slugger had a deal with a company harvesting the wood in a secret location in Europe, the wood then being taken to another European country for a clandestine two-stage, six-month kiln drying process. The hush-hush atmosphere was simply H & B and its supplier playing hardball in an increasingly competitive bat-making environment. (Even Louisville Slugger's executives didn't know how this new drying worked, and workers in each of the two stages didn't know exactly what the other group did.) But suddenly the company's supply dried up and beech operations had to be suspended. Given the inherent costs of getting trees from overseas and the fact that Louisville Slugger wasn't getting enough demand from other players, it abandoned the project. On the other end of the business spectrum, an American baseball coach named Andy Weissman undertook the quixotic effort to build demand for bats made from Ukranian beech, but his tiny company, Ya Ya Bats, has yet to establish a presence in America, getting only European, Cuban, and Venezuelan teams to use some of the 4,000 bats he makes per year. But Don Fine, who owns Viper Bats and several other companies, is still pursuing European Beech. He has a supplier in Germany, who does the two-step process—steam drying and then kiln drying—and Fine says he is exploring whether the major obstacles—the cost of making and importing the bats—can be overcome.

The best hope for a new wood seems to be yellow birch. "Some players feel maple is too rigid and like the whip you can get with ash, and yellow birch is right in between," says Michel Laplante, founder of B45, generally considered the first company to use yellow birch.

Jeff McKee, vice-president of Trinity Bats says birch is more affordable to make because the moisture content can be higher than maple. "We've had cases where we had to order 500 logs to make 12 bats from maple." He adds that birch's longer fiber lengths make it more flexible, so that when a birch bat does break, "there's an 80 percent chance it stays together." Given its unique characteristics, many of the most popular Trinity birch models feature medium-size handles, while most maple bat-makers are touting their super skinny handles. "Why buy those when you already know the outcome?" McKee asks.

Don Fine, who split off a separate company, Birch Bats, from his other brands, believes birch will continue growing in popularity; D-Bat founder Cade Griffis agrees, but says it is has been slow going. "Four years ago birch looked like it was going to take off and it still hasn't," he says, since players are often reluctant to try new things. "Still, I think it will eventually catch on."

Beyond birch, the search continues, says Jim Wells of Mattingly Sports. "There's a subspecies of hickory I've been looking at in Africa and in the swamps of Louisiana," he says. "And there are lots of other things out there. I'm thinking about trying to go higher up the tree to get the wood."

While there has been much made of the maple movement, the baseball bat revolution—after decades of stasis—now is even returning from the search for new woods back to changing the shape of the bat itself. Baseball is built on tradition, so change comes slowly if at all. The earliest innovations in bat-making—the double knob for batters who hit with their hands apart, the mushroom knob—disappeared quickly. In 1906 a man named Emile Kinst patented a bat with small grooves and a flat concave curve near the barrel, where it met up with other grooves, enabling batters to drive the ball in different directions. Of course, that put it in violation of major league rules calling for a smooth, round surface, and the bat disappeared without becoming a hit. In the 1970s Illinois businessman John Bennett created a bent broom and, when he saw how much easier the new angle was on his arm, moved on to bent hammers, fishing rods, tennis rackets, and…baseball bats. Bennett's bats featured a 19-degree bend. By pointing the bent part at the pitcher, the batter was less likely to roll his wrists and could snap the bat around more quickly. (A similar "banana bat" had been patented in 1890.) Bennett got Louisville Slugger to take a look at his model, and the company showed it to some members of the Big Red Machine. A slumping Johnny Bench took a chance on it and went on a tear, which prompted major league officials to quash its use. College baseball banned it too, but Hillerich & Bradsby eventually created an aluminum version of the bat called the Big Bend.

A handful of today's bat-makers continue to look for ways to improve upon the bat, though they do it in ways that are less of a sharp break with tradition. Akadema broke into the baseball business glove-first, introducing unique redesigns in that tradition-bound field. Founders Lawrence and Joe Gilligan turned to bats next, launching a line hand-turned by Amish craftsmen working without electricity. (Today it makes many bats the old-fashioned way but also some in-house with modern amenities.) The main innovation came with its Tacktion, which features a mixture of walnut shells, sunflower seeds, and sand ground into the handle to provide a built-in grip.

But the most dramatic changes have come from two companies, one with the imprimatur of a great hitter, the other from a company that had spent decades making balls, not bats.

From 1984 to 1986, Don Mattingly amassed more hits than anyone else in baseball. In the 1980s the New York Yankee first baseman also finished in the American League top five in total bases four times and RBI five times. In other words, the man could hit. At the start of the 21st century, he returned to the show as a coach and then the manager of the Dodgers. But it's what Donnie Baseball did away from the bigs in that decade that may have his greatest impact on the game: creating a bat that teaches young hitters proper technique. His Mattingly V-Grip Bat is flat along two sides of the handle, creating a V to help hitters keep the bat in their fingers instead of their palms, leading to a quicker swing with more snap.

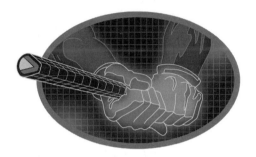

Photo Credit: Mattingly Sports

In 2005, former New York Yankee great Don Mattingly introduced the first major innovation to the shape of the bat in decades, a V-shaped grip designed to keep the handle in the hitter's fingers, quicken his swing, and get the bat head out front without the wrists rolling.

"I was watching my kids play, going to all their tournaments and seeing kids swing with the bat squashed in their hand and their elbow out sideways," Mattingly says. "I thought, 'Man, the swing is not supposed to look like that.'"

Mattingly decided that the bat itself was partly to blame for the faulty mechanics. Many young players clutched the bat in the palm of their hand instead of up in their fingers, but even those who started correctly had the bat roll into the palm during the swing. He thought back to clearing out his father-in-law's woods with an axe the year before he reached the majors and how "chopping down trees transformed my cut into a power swing." But Mattingly, who always scraped down his bat handles, didn't think a pure axe handle would cut it—without some roundness, it would hurt the hitter's hands. (Someone had sold an axe handle bat in the 1980s but the idea whiffed.) So he started "messing around, trying to get angles that would create the snap and get the bat out in the hitter's fingers."

Then Mattingly met Jim Wells, who, like Mattingly, was from Indiana. Mattingly showed the lumber industry veteran his idea, thinking that it might make a good training bat. He also told Wells he didn't want to get involved in a bat company. Wells made a model and Mattingly suggested some minor tweaks; within weeks Wells was back with a prototype. Before testing it on his sons, Mattingly decided to try the bat himself. Wells uses the word "epiphany" to describe the moment he first found the right angles for what is now the Mattingly V-Grip Bat, and the ex-Yankee had the same experience. "It was kind of instant," he says. "When I swung the bat I thought, 'This is not just for training. This is a real bat. Why wouldn't you use it in a game?'"

Mattingly was interested in taking this beyond just his sons' teams. "This wouldn't be just any old bat company, I'd be teaching and helping guys become better players," Mattingly says. That was in 2004 and Mattingly knew that a generation of aluminum bat use followed by another of steroid use had enabled players to become sluggers without proper technique. "Now there's going to be more emphasis on technique and kids need to understand how to hit."

Mattingly is a baseball man, not a businessman, but on a plane ride he met someone who knew about running a company. Skip Shaw had just retired from a managing partner position at the consulting company Accenture. "One of the first questions Skip asked me was whether this was a business or a hobby," Mattingly recalls. A year later, Mattingly Sports was born, with Shaw providing the nuts-and-bolts knowledge needed to build a company up from the grassroots. "It doesn't matter how good the bat is if we can't get it in people's hands," Mattingly says.

Shaw set about getting youth and amateur leagues to approve a non-cylindrical bat (the rule is really aimed at keeping the barrel round), seeding the bats in tournaments and leagues to create demand for retailers, using social media to drum up interest, and of course capitalizing on the Mattingly's name in getting the media's attention, especially in New York. "One major advantage we have is that the bat was invented by one of the greatest hitters," Shaw says, adding that Mattingly is more than a celebrity name for the company and has never missed a board meeting, even if he has to participate by phone while traveling as manager of the Dodgers. (Shaw has also pushed the company forward to ensure it's not a one-hit wonder, with new innovations like the Balistk, with a one-piece composite interior and an aluminum sheath.)

The three men are not sure if the V-Grip will ever be used in major league games (although some players use it as a practice bat), especially, Wells says, because MLB might make them share their patented technology. Still, since he says the V-Grip "makes you hit with the strongest grain every time, and the safety factor could warrant MLB looking at it and it might be worth it to us one day."

Photo Credit: Baden Sports

Axe Bat offers a new handle, one shaped like an axe, that its makers say automatically gets the hitter's hands into the proper swinging position.

But the V-Grip is not the only game-changer out there. Two years ago Baden Sports introduced another twist in the straight-handled bat world with its Axe Bat. This family owned-business has been around since 1979, specializing in balls for different sports. It had never ventured over to the bat side. But one day sales manager Rusty Trudeau received a bat sent to him by an inventor. (The man behind the Axe Bat wishes to remain anonymous, Trudeau says.) Unlike the failed ax-shaped bat of the 1980s, which had a crooked handle, this had more curve for the batter's hands.

"As an old coach I could see the benefit of it right away—the handle automatically sets your hands in the correct position to keep them from prematurely rolling, so you swing 'palm up, palm down,'" Trudeau recalls. But he adds that "Being a traditionalist myself, I just thought, 'No way.'"

The first prototype of the Axe Bat sat by Trudeau's desk for weeks. But he kept picking it up and holding it in his hands. The feel of the bat eventually wore down his resistance. And the purist in Trudeau saw that in the baseball bible (a.k.a. *The Science of Hitting*) by the great deity of batting, Ted Williams, the Splendid Splinter proclaimed that swinging a bat was like hitting an axe into a tree—a batter wants to make contact before he rolls his wrists. Getting this moment of impact right could help a hitter make more solid contact and produce more power. And so in 2009, the Axe was born.

Despite the Baden name, Trudeau says plenty of sporting goods dealers as well as players were initially gun-shy, just as he had been. "At shows or tournaments, you'd get a look of 'What the heck,'" he says. "People think it's a gimmick. But once they put it in their hands, those who truly know hitting get it right away."

By 2010 the knobless wonder was not only approved by amateur organizations like Little League and the NCAA but also by MLB, making it the first non-round bat ever approved. (The company hopes to have major leaguers swinging the Axe in games in 2012.)

In addition to keeping the bat in the fingers and preventing the wrists from rolling early, Trudeau says the handle allows for a "non-restricted release," pointing to many hitters who hold their pinky over the knob or choke up on the bat to get away from the knob altogether. (Thus the axe handle could reduce hammate bone injuries suffered by hitters.) Like the V-Grip, the Axe also forces hitters to make contact with the strongest part of the bat, reducing the number of broken bats.

The company makes no round-handled bats, believing it would be hypocritical, Trudeau says. "Why would we endorse the old way when we're saying this is better?" And anyway, adds Max Kay, the company's vice-president of development and operations, the old concept—a round handle, with a knob—"was a historical accident." The bats were designed that way, he argues, because lathes could only make symmetrical pieces and the knobs were there initially for turning the wood. Now that there are computerized lathes capable of creating bats with handles more naturally suited to hitting, Kay asks, "Why not do it that way?"

Chapter 8

THE SLUGGER FROM LOUISVILLE
The Granddaddy of Bat-Makers

> When I got to the big leagues,
> I got my bat and it had my signature on it.
> It was a lousy signature, but it was a Louisville Slugger
> and I felt like I had arrived.
>
> *Tony Gwynn*

The bat is such a part of classic Americana it even has its own creation myth.

Bats may have been continually evolving, but for more than 125 years there has been one constant in the field: the Louisville Slugger. Here's the legend. In 1884 Pete "The Gladiator" Browning, who played for the Louisville Eclipse and was one of the leading sluggers in the American Association, broke his favorite bat one day. John "Bud" Hillerich, the 17-year-old son of a local woodworker, happened to be there and told Browning, "Come on over and I'll make you a new bat."

On a lathe, Hillerich shaped a stick from white ash as Browning offered tips. The next day, Browning went 3-for-3. Over the objections of Bud's dad, J. Frederich, the teenager began filling requests from Browning's teammates, making bats and eventually making history.

It's a great story, featuring one of the most colorful characters of early baseball. Browning was partially deaf and a heavy drinker. He'd been a local marbles champion before becoming a baseball star, and he retained his quirky side, occasionally balancing on one leg to catch the ball or refusing to slide into a base. According to Bob Hill's *Crack of the Bat*, he notated his hits on his shirt cuff, named his bats (Mary, Joe, even Lazarus) and retired them after each achieved a certain number of hits.

However, Hill points out, this tale seems to be just that, a tale…and a tall one at that. Browning never mentioned the incident, nor did any contem-

OLD JUDGE CIGARETTES   Goodwin & Co., New York.

Photo Credit: Library of Congress, LC-DIG-bbc-0580f

Louisville Slugger's creation myth starts in 1884 with a teenaged Bud Hillerich hand-crafting a new bat for local slugger Pete Browning.

porary features or his obituary. In a 1914 interview, Bud Hillerich made it seem that he merely carved a ring around the superstitious star's lumber (which was reportedly 37 inches and a whopping 48 ounces). Browning also said he had made his own bat then lent it to a player named Gus Weyhing, who helped spread the word. A third baseman for the St. Louis Browns in the 1880s named Arnie Latham claimed decades later to have been the recipient of the first Hillerich bat. There are other variations on the story, with the elder Hillerich making a bat for either Browning (or more convincingly for his own son's budding baseball career), then grudgingly consenting to carve more for other players as word of mouth spread. But the Browning story stuck because the Louisville Slugger marketing folks began pushing it and embellishing the details in the late 1930s and 1940s.

Even though the true creation story of the Louisville Slugger will likely never be known, by the mid-1880s the Hillerich family was in the bat business, way ahead of the proverbial curve. But J. Frederich Hillerich was initially reluctant to fill bat orders. After all, why worry about accessories for a frivolous game when your business is built on making a solid and reliable staple: the swinging butter churn (not to mention the bed posts, roller skids, and even wooden bowling balls the company made). This modern marvel, also called the "dairy swing churn," allowed customers to convert milk to butter by

Photo Credit: Louisville Slugger Museum & Factory

While Bud Hillerich (in doorway, holding a bat) fell in love with bat-making, his father J. Frederich (second from left, with a beard but no bat) resisted the notion at first, preferring instead to stick with making products like the butter churn (at Bud's feet).

rocking the churn back and forth instead of having to exert the energy needed to beat it up and down.

There was only so much time and manpower available for production, and the elder Hillerich preferred devoting it to the churn. But by the 1890s, the company was "Hillerich & Son," and the younger generation preferred batters to butter. In a photo of the factory's workers, Frederich the Founder is empty-handed, but Bud, the company's future, stands in the doorway, wielding a bat. An 1895 ad that touted both butter churns and bats made by this wood-turning company seemed to delineate the internecine struggle, but the tilt already had begun toward bats. The bats earned a new moniker along the way. First simply called the "Hillerich" bat and then the "Falls City Slugger" (for the nearby Ohio River's rapids), by 1894 the company bat had been patented as the "Louisville Slugger." However, the company still sold most of its bats as private label deals with companies like Rawlings and Montgomery Ward; it also sold its own inexpensive Buster Brown line.

The Hillerich & Son factory didn't stand alone, of course. Yes, Willie Keeler, John McGraw, and others hoisted the Slugger at home plate, but there were dozens of rivals, including companies like the Michigan-based Pontiac Turning Company, which had a Native American in full regalia as its logo (Frank Chance sported these bats) and the A.J. Reach company (started by a former major leaguer and founder of the Philadelphia Phillies). Meanwhile, Cap Anson and Buck Ewing preferred bats from the firm of A.G. Spalding, an ex-ballplayer turned entrepreneur. Spalding sold not only its Gold Medal Bat, with a special finish but also what it claimed was a vital innovation with its "mushroom bat." Designed by the company's bat-maker, Jack Pickett, the newcomer featured an oversized knob on the handle that was supposed to offer better balance. Meanwhile, the Wright and Ditson company (co-founded by George Wright, baseball's earliest professional star) produced the double-ring-handle model—a short-lived gimmick that provided a knob for each hand for players who held their hands apart and slapped at the ball. (The slap tactic was favored by Honus Wagner and Ty Cobb, among others.) For players who choked up, this bat gave them a knob near their grip. A more significant innovation was the marketing of the bat: The company got Cleveland star Nap Lajoie to endorse it, proclaiming, "a better grip thus more confidence which means a better and higher salary."

Photo Credit: Phoenix Bats

The Louisville Slugger faced constant competition. Nap Lajoie briefly endorsed a rival's double-ring handle for slap hitters made by professional baseball pioneer George Wright's company.

Facing such aggressive competition, the younger Hillerich first patented a process for hardening the bat's surface to prevent it from chipping or splintering. Then he hit upon an even more important idea, a marketing ploy that topped Wright and Ditson's. On September 1, 1905, the Louisville company signed Honus Wagner, Pittsburgh's star shortstop, to an endorsement contract and burned a copy of his autograph into the wood barrel of the bat. This innovation would be as important as the bats themselves, as millions of boys over the next century dreamed of having a professional bat with their own name emblazoned on it.

Other early bat signees were Cobb of the Detroit Tigers, perennial home run leader Harry Davis of the Philadelphia A's, and none other than Lajoie, who defected from Wright and Ditson. Eddie Collins and Home Run Baker, both also of the A's, were next to sign up.

Cobb actually passed up the $75 endorsement payment for the right to oversee the hand-turning of his bats and to have his own private bin at the plant. In today's dollars, modern players don't get much more than Cobb was offered because the company signs many minor leagues who won't ever see the majors. (The company has given extra incentives to established stars, awarding Hank Aaron $7,000 when he approached home run No. 700.) But players who sign with Louisville know they're getting premium timber meticulously crafted (Wagner got his tinted a deep red) and their own signature on a Louisville Slugger. It is a true sign they have reached the big time. (Most players, even major leaguers, have their names only in block letters if they don't have a contract with the company.)

The original Hillerich factory burned down in 1910 (although that year's billets were saved, as were the model bats for players like Wagner and Cobb) and the rebuilt one was the only factory in America devoted exclusively to making bats. Its presence made clear that the Hillerich clan had settled on its identity.

Still, although Louisville Slugger is an American classic today, the bat-making plant easily could have been just another small company that eventually faded away. The game-changer was Frank Bradsby, who joined the Slugger team in 1911 after working as a buyer for Simmons Hardware, which was one of the bat company's top retail partners. While Bud Hillerich knew all the

Photo Credit: Louisville Slugger Museum & Factory

The greatest marketing move in bat-making history came when Louisville Slugger started offering different models "autographed" by major league stars. The company's Signature Wall is filled with All-Stars and Hall of Famers.

players—and kept files with cards detailing what kind of bats each man preferred. Bradsby was a shrewd salesman and savvy marketer. After the fire, he helped rescue the company and was soon Bud Hillerich's equal—by 1916, the company had been renamed Hillerich & Bradsby (also called H & B), which is still its official name today, although most people know the company by its most famous bat's name. In fact J. Frederich Hillerich trusted Bradsby more than he did his own son, selling off a controlling interest to Bradsby, who had the sense to understand Bud Hillerich's contributions. Bradsby hired Bud as president and then sold him back a portion of the business.

Bradsby quickly shifted the company away from the private label sales and the Buster Brown model to an emphasis on the Louisville Slugger brand.

In 1914 he introduced Louisville Slugger Juniors for kids, and in 1919 he kicked off an ambitious campaign aimed at the retail market. (Most of the other bat companies—there were 28 competitors by then—already had budgeted money for national advertising.) The multi-pronged attack featured famous Slugger pamphlets and the slogan, "Ask the batboy—he knows," which ran in ads with photos showing major league batboys in bat-related conversation with various stars.

Bradsby's timing was perfect. As the Jazz Age dawned and Babe Ruth took center stage in New York, bat sales soared. By 1923, 1.68 million total bats had been sold in America, up from 276,000 in 1919. Louisville Slugger alone sold 600,000 in 1923, up from 144,000 in 1919, with autographed-model sales jumping from about half to 80 percent of the company's sales. Babe Ruth, Ty Cobb, and George Sisler of the St. Louis Browns were the most popular names on those bats, but the name that mattered most was Louisville Slugger, which solidified its position as America's premier bat-maker.

The strong bond between Hillerich & Bradsby and the ballplayers was further enhanced by the loyalty employees seemed to feel for the company. Even today, many of the staff, particularly those working in the factory, measure their time there in decades, not years. Henry Morrow started out in the company in 1901 by sweeping floors, but he rose to plant foreman and point man to the pros. Morrow traveled to spring training, and on weekends during the season he visited St. Louis and Chicago, where he could see every team play. He sized up potential new players to sign and chatted up the stars about what they wanted for their bats. Morrow stayed with the company until 1946.

When Ted Williams of the Red Sox went to Louisville as a young slugger and began searching through the woodpiles for the perfect lumber, he established an instant kinship with veteran bat-maker Fritz Bickel. Fritz's father Henry had worked for the Hilleriches from 1881 (before they began making bats) through 1938. The younger Fritz went to work at the company in 1912, six years before Williams was born, and he stayed until 1962, two years after Williams retired. (When Williams enhanced their relationship with a $10 tip, the Spendid Splinter knew he'd be in good hands for years afterward.) Henry Bickel's nephew Augie also worked for H & B for 42 years. And the current bat guru, Danny Luckett, shares the Bickels' dedication to the job. He has been

Photo Credit: Louisville Slugger Museum & Factory

Danny Luckett is the current master of bat making at Louisville Slugger—he follows in the company's grand tradition, not just of overseeing production personally but of doing it for decades.

there for 42 years and counting.

By the 1940s Louisville Slugger's stature had grown exponentially, as had sales. The company began offering curious fans factory tours in the 1930s, and by 1940 it was selling two million bats a year. Louisville Slugger found its way into the hands of 90 percent of all big leaguers, along with many Negro leaguers. By 1956 sales reached three million annually; a decade later, after passing the historic 100-million total lifetime production in 1960, the annual output soared past four million.

As the bat business—and Hillerich & Bradsby's sideline in golf clubs—soared, the company began to run out of room. New president John A. Hillerich III undertook a secret search for a new factory. In 1972, with business at a peak and more than six million Sluggers being made every year, Hillerich found a site just four miles away from the existing plant—a 114,000-square-foot building originally designed for woodworking on 60 acres of land. There was one huge problem, however: The site wasn't in Louisville; in fact it wasn't even in Kentucky.

That didn't stop John Hillerich. That October, he loaded all his employees onto buses for a mystery tour to show them their new home. Halfway across the Ohio River, on their way into Indiana, publicist Jack McGrath turned to Hillerich and said, "My God, do you know what you've done?"

To quell talk of a name change to the "Indiana Slugger," Hillerich kept the company address and headquarters in Louisville. Still, in the long run, the change was not meant to be. Hillerich once defended the move by saying, "It was a very good business decision." But, he added, "...I don't think I'd do it again."

Hillerich also made a bad business decision in not taking the rise of aluminum bats seriously enough. When they first became popular in the 1970s after being approved for play from Little League up through college, Hillerich & Bradsby followed companies like Easton and Worth into the field, but the company merely churned out low cost products instead of trying to be innovative.

By the 1990s aluminum bats had thoroughly wormed their way into the baseball world, eating into H & B's wood-bat production, which dropped from seven million annually to around a million. (It has since picked up a bit, and the company makes 1.8 million a year—including souvenir bats. The company still makes over 100,000 bats a year for minor leaguers and 86,000 for major leaguers.) However, the company finally began playing catch-up on the metal bat side, and these days Hillerich & Bradsby makes most of its profits off aluminum bats and ancillary businesses. Because the aluminum bats were made in California, the company no longer needed the mammoth space in Indiana and the prodigal factory returned to Louisville.

Initial plans for a new facility called for a 270-foot steel bat to be erected with an elevator and observation deck, but that outsized idea was soon abandoned. Today, the offices, factory, and Louisville Slugger Museum & Factory are housed in a handsome replica of an old red brick Civil War warehouse. The museum and factory tours draw 230,000 visitors a year. The exhibits were renovated in 2009, and the displays include an explanation of the bat-making process, plenty of bats (from quirky, failed experiments to a bat Babe Ruth used in 1927), and the biggest hit, so to speak—the Hold a Piece of History exhibit where visitors don white cotton gloves and get to hold a bat that was used in a game by players such as Mickey Mantle, Cal Ripken, Jr., and Johnny Bench. And, of course, there's a batting cage that—unlike most cages today, which use aluminum bats—offers up different wooden models hitters can choose to swing.

The Louisville Slugger Museum & Factory draws nearly a quarter of a million visitors annually to see how bats are made and to explore baseball history.

The museum is hard to miss—it's the only building in town with a 120-foot sculpture of a bat leaning against it. Built from carbon steel, the bat weighs 68,000 pounds and is nine feet in diameter at the base and three and a half feet at the handle. The steel was covered with five layers of paint, including a hand-painted wood-grain outer layer for a genuine wood look. Engineered, fabricated, and painted by local companies, the bat took 1,500 man-hours over six months to build and paint. The bat leans at 11½ degrees into the building and is supported by concrete piles and a 5,000-pound weight that was placed inside the bat just below the knob (to guard against major windstorms).

Erected in 1995, the bat is an R43 model, which was designed for Babe Ruth but here features the signature of "Bud Hillerich" in homage to the bat-making pioneer.

Chapter 9

NOW BATTING...
Louisville Sluggers' bat-making rivals

**I couldn't make a better ash tree,
and I knew there was more than one way to make a bat.**

Sam Holman,
founder of the Original Maple Bat Corporation and Sam Bats

In the first half of the 20th century, Hillerich & Bradsby's Louisville Slugger outmarketed and outlasted all its early competitors.

By the early 1940s, 90% of all bats swung by major leaguers were Louisville Sluggers. But while the Slugger remains the most powerful force in baseball bats to this day, other companies have carved out notable positions in the field.

In the tiny town of Dolgeville, for example, deep in the heart of northern white ash territory in upstate New York, a guy named Edwin McLaughlin started a sawmill and factory. McLaughlin's work included producing billets for bat-makers, which gave McLaughlin and another man, Charles Millard, an idea. In 1946 the duo began making their own bats from local wood, which they named Adirondack bats.

Dolgeville, it turns out, was also the hometown of Hal Schumacher, a longtime pitcher for the New York Giants. From 1933 through 1942, Schumacher won over 150 games, including 61 wins over the first three years. But he missed three seasons for World War II and when he returned in 1946, he was 35 and pretty much done, going 4-4 in that last season. Schmacher may have been a pitcher, but he'd slammed a respectable 15 homers in 896 at-bats in the major leagues and, of course, he was a local boy with big-time connections. He signed on with Adirondack as its major league liaison. Before he died, Bobby Thomson recalled in an interview that in the spring of 1947, "Schumacher walked into the [Giants] locker room with I don't know how many dozens of

Adirondack's Big Stick has been swung through the years by everyone from Johnny Mize to Roberto Clemente to Matt Kemp. It is always instantly recognizable thanks to its Pro Ring at the top of the handle.

Adirondack bats." Enticed by free samples, most Giants started using the new sticks. New York had hit 121 home runs in the 1946 N.L. season, but the Giants pounded out a then-record 221 homers in 1947 with their new weapons. The Giants' Johnny Mize tied Pittsburgh's Ralph Kiner for the league lead with 51, and three of Mize's teammates—Willard Marshall (36), Walker Cooper (35), and Thomson (29)—rounded out the N.L.'s top five home run hitters. (Thomson said Cooper—"who hit the hardest balls I ever saw"—was so enamored of his new Adirondack bat that when it started chipping, he drove nails into it to preserve it, until he got caught.)

The Adirondack bat emerged as the main challenger to Louisville Slugger over the next few decades as such stars as Willie Mays, Roberto Clemente, Willie McCovey, Joe Torre, Reggie Jackson, and Mike Schmidt swung the Big Stick with its distinctive Pro Ring. The original families sold to corporate interests in the 1960s, and the company eventually merged to become part of Rawlings Sporting Goods in 1975, which still owns it today, cranking out about 400,000 Adirondacks annually (including about 5,000 for major leaguers and 25,000 for minor leaguers). Troy Tulowitzki, Joe Mauer, and Matt Kemp are among the current players swinging a Big Stick. However, Rawlings was bought in 2003 by K2, a corporate conglomerate that since then has also snapped up Miken Bats and Worth Sports. (Worth had started making wood bats in 1969 and had its banner year in 1988 when Jose Canseco used its sticks in his 40-homer, 40-steal season and Kirk Gibson used one to launch perhaps the most famous pinch-hit home run in baseball history.)

The other major company to challenge Louisville Slugger comes from a nation on the other side of the planet that shares our passion for the sport. Most

Americans probably underestimate the depth of the roots of baseball in Japan, thinking it traces back to—at the earliest—the barnstorming tours of Babe Ruth and Lou Gehrig in the 1930s. But baseball had taken hold much earlier. In fact in 1906 kimono-shop worker Rihachi Mizuno and his younger brother Rizo opened a baseball equipment store in Osaka and, before long, Mizuno sponsored baseball tournaments, added a factory, and began making the equipment.

Although Rihachi Mizuno had to suspend operations during World War II to make war-related goods, the factory returned to its sporting goods production immediately thereafter. Mizuno continually innovated. For instance, the company injected resin into wooden bats to make them more durable.

In 1959 Mizuno hired Isokazu Kubota to work in the factory in the town of Yoro. "I was only looking for someplace close enough to commute to. I got this job completely by chance," Kubota said. Yet once there, he stayed for a half-century and became Mizuno's reigning master bat-maker. He custom-shaves bats down by hand after an initial turn by a modern machine. And Kubota uses his carpenter's shaver without the aid of a tape measure, although he keeps a scale handy to weigh the bats. His attention to detail became renowned—for Ichiro Suzuki's bats he shaves off an extra-quarter ounce of wood so the lacquer doesn't add anything to the final weight.

The billion-dollar company is still run by Rihachi's descendants and maintains its reputation for innovation. But Mizuno's presence no longer is limited to Japan. Beginning with a deal with Pete Rose in 1978, Mizuno's bats—some made from Japanese trees, others from American—have become increasingly popular in the majors, especially in recent years with such Japanese stars (and Kubota clients) as Suzuki and Hideki Matsui proving themselves in the bigs.

In the 1990s a new wave of boutique bat-makers took to the lathe, with the products of such companies as Glomar, Kissimmee, Hoosier Bats, and Carolina Clubs reaching the major leagues. Many, like Glomar and Kissimmee, have since been sold off (the former was recently bought back by the original owners, the latter was sold to Easton), while a few of the sturdier companies, such as Carolina, have survived. The cost of doing business has grown exponentially since then says Carolina Clubs co-founder Kevin Lane: "Our new equipment can turn a bat every 38 seconds, but the machine costs

Photo Credit: Carolina Clubs

At smaller companies, like Carolina Clubs, it really is a hands-on business. Here co-owner Kevin Lane examines the wood that will be transformed into bats.

$200,000, where our first machine cost $800-$1,000."

Carolina Clubs started out like Louisville Slugger— accidentally and as a family business. In the early 1990s, Kevin and Tom Lane were struggling minor leaguers who knew that to make it to The Show might require an alternate route. So they asked their father, George, who was running a staircase-making company, if he could make them a bat. Intrigued, George set up a lathe in a tool shed that once had stored his boys' bicycles. When his sons' teammates were impressed with George's stick, the Lane boys figured they were onto something—and soon an enterprise was born.

The Florida-based company received approval to make bats for professional ball from MLB in 1992, and within five years it got a big boost when Ryan Klesko went on a home run tear—a spree he credited to the Lanes' "Carolina Club." (The boys' mother, Mickie, had hoped to retire to the Carolinas, but George's respiratory ailments thwarted that plan. So the sons named the company in honor of her dream.)

Carolina remains a family business—older sister Karen also is a full-time employee—although the company, with its "No Cork Needed" slogan, expanded as other players reached stardom. (Bobby Abreu started swinging a Carolina Club in Class A ball.) In 2004, Hillerich & Bradsby, which had supplied wood to many smaller bat-makers, cut off the little guys. Carolina Club survived by purchasing its own mill in upstate New York (it also has two production facilities) and continues producing more than 15,000 bats each year.

Among the recent start-ups the biggest name is also one of the shortest names: The Sam Bat. The Sam Bat story starts like this: A guy walks into a bar.... Sounds like a classic setup line for a joke, but it's also the birth of the biggest revolution in wooden baseball bats since the Hillerichs gave up the butter churn.

The guy in question was Sam Holman, a woodcarver and longtime stage-hand for Canada's National Arts Centre. The bar was The Mayflower, in Holman's hometown of Ottawa, where Holman saw a familiar face, that of Bill MacKenzie, a Colorado Rockies scout who had just returned from spring training. MacKenzie was grumbling about the number of bats players had broken. Holman was not a huge baseball fan, but he did love talking wood. The scout issued a challenge: Could Holman design a bat that wouldn't break?

Holman pored over everything from *The Physics of Baseball* to the *Standard Handbook for Civil Engineers*, plus the 200-plus existing bat patents. All those patents dealt with ash bats, and Holman knew there was no dramatic way to improve on those.

But Ottawa is surrounded by forest land, and Holman was knowledge-able about Canadian maple. The wood has a tighter grain and is denser and stronger than ash, but it also is unpredictable and therefore more difficult to deal with. Historically, bat companies had shied away from maple. Holman knew that modern kiln-drying techniques could enable him to use maple effectively. (His bats dry to a moisture content of just 7 to 9 percent.) So in 1996

Holman, working with MacKenzie as an adviser, bought a rare Italian lathe (used for making ax handles), converted his basement/garage into a workshop, took a leftover part of a maple banister from a home renovation, and carved the maple into a bat.

Holman founded the Original Maple Bat Corporation, and his first bats were called the Rideau Crusher, named in part for a noted Canadian waterway, although he later changed the name to Sam Bats. With financial support from his sister, Holman formally launched the company in 1997. He had his brother Nathan design the logo of a flying bat (the animal kind).

Photo Credit: Sam Bats

Sam Holman hefts one of his maple bats, made famous by Barry Bonds in his record-setting 73 home run campaign on 2001. The logo in the center is a bat—the flying kind.

After players on the Class AAA Ottawa Lynx tried his experimental bat, Holman improved the design and then finagled a meeting with Joe Carter, Carlos Delgado, and Ed Sprague, all playing at the time for the Toronto Blue Jays. The players tried the bat in batting practice, and Carter especially liked the new wood. He gave Holman more tips and later became Holman's first major league customer, sneaking a bat into a game and homering in 1997. (The bats were not authorized by MLB until 1998.)

But it was another customer who would be most responsible for the success of Sam Bats and, to a great extent, the surge in all maple bat sales. In 1999 Barry Bonds met Holman and agreed to take a few batting practice swings with the carpenter's creation. Like Carter, Bonds liked the hard wood but had some advice. So he and Holman shifted the barrel weight and fattened the knob, eventually fashioning the weapon that Bonds would wield in 2001, the year he smashed a record 73 home runs.

While the "cream" and the "clear" probably had plenty to do with Bonds' newfound power, the San Francisco slugger preferred publicly focusing attention on his new wood. After that, Sam Bats took off like a ball crushed by Bonds.

Holman moved his business from his basement/garage into a former bar (a place that once served as a brothel). The new location gave him more than 20 times the space of his old work station, and his staff grew from two to twelve—not counting the workshop people who turned the larger blanks into rounds ready to go on the lathe. By 2005 Holman was up to 17,000 bats. The maple manifesto was the real deal. Today, Sam Bats makes 17,000-20,000 bats a year, and over 100 major leaguers including Ryan Braun, Troy Tulowitzki, and Miguel Cabrera wield Holman's sticks. (Despite the endless controversy surrounding Bonds, his model bat remains popular and sales have actually increased over time.) Still, making money wasn't easy for a small company—at one point in 2006 Holman tried selling the entire company for $3.5 million on ebay, but no one bid on it. Bonds eventually kicked in $40,000 and Holman found other four private investors to keep the company and its employees going. (Holman is now a minority shareholder and remains active in the company but not in the daily operations.)

Despite the financial risks, after Holman hit it big, an entire wave of do-it-yourselfers went "batty." From Superior Bats in upstate New York to D-Bats in Texas, new companies popped up from sea to shining sea—and some of these bat-makers became extremely popular with big leaguers. Soon enough, however, Major League Baseball decided it had too much of a good thing. With 48 licensed bat-makers—up from just 11 five years earlier—there was a steady stream of bat salesmen pitching their wares to ballplayers and driving the team equipment managers crazy. MLB went from doing nothing about this to an overreaction, creating excessive insurance premiums and other requirements that forced about three-quarters of the companies out of the game. Most smaller companies say Louisville Slugger feared the competition and prompted the sport to take action. (Many players are not faithful to one company and switch between two or three different bats.)

After an outcry from the smaller companies and some of the players, MLB modified its stance and devised midrange requirements so that today there are 31 approved bat manufacturers. Still the cost of playing ball with the big boys keeps going up for the little guys.

Charles "Lefty" Trudeau, founder of Phoenix Bats is unhappy with the fees, but says that having Miguel Cabrera swing the bat and show it to younger ballplayers helps justify the cost. "It's difficult to make the case that you're selling a high quality bat if it isn't being used at the highest levels of the game," says Jack Kasarjian, owner of X Bats, which took off in 2002 when it went from two major leaguers to 86 using its bats, helped by a *Sports Illustrated* photo that featured Mike Lieberthal hefting one. (After Sammy Sosa and Manny Ramirez began using X Bats, it caught on with other Latinos. The company now boasts that as many as 300 major leaguers swing an X Bat.) Still, plenty of companies have dropped out of the pro game, saying it's not worth it. "It just became too expensive," says Akadema co-founder Joe Gilligan. "I'm making much more money now that I'm not spending the money for their fees."

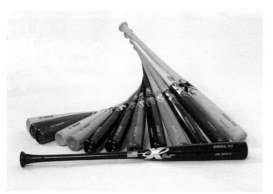

Photo Credit: X Bats

Despite new regulations and increasing fees and insurance premiums imposed by Major League Baseball many small companies, like X Bats, continue to shell out big bucks to gain the exposure that comes from having big leaguers swinging their sticks.

"We decided to attack the retail market more aggressively instead of spending that money, which was $50,000 the first year," says Kevin Lane of Carolina Clubs, adding that he might one day return to the MLB game.

Still, whether they're making the bats for major leaguers, minor leaguers or Little Leaguers, there are dozens of bat companies out there, striving for their share of the crowded marketplace.

The companies often have unusual origin stories, with many starting either accidentally or on a whim. The Minnesota-based Glacial Wood Products is among the nation's largest custom wood-turning companies and initially ventured into the bat arena by creating product for X Bat. But after that business relationship soured, Glacial Wood owner Richard Johnson decided to stay in the bat business by teaming up Jim Anderson, a local entrepreneur who had founded tiny MaxBat out of his basement workshop. (The company is named after his son). Anderson, a woodworker and veteran amateur ballplayer, had been making bats for players in his adult league. After the terrorist attacks of 9/11/01, he yearned to spend his days doing something he really loved, so he quit his job selling newspaper advertising to pursue bat-making. The marriage with Glacial Wood was perfect. "I needed someone to produce the bat and they needed someone to sell and market it," Anderson says. Today MaxBat operates independently out of the original Glacial Wood facility (after Glacial Wood moved two miles to the east) and has eight full-time employees. Anderson says that there are 100-150 major leaguers swinging a MaxBat, and the company is making 30,000 bats per year and growing, yet it works hard to remain small at heart, making all bats to customer specifications. (Any wood that doesn't meet its criteria is relegated to being used for trophy bats.)

Old Hickory Bat Company was founded in 1999 but traces its roots to the pre-maple days of the early 1990s when Jon Moyer, created the KC Slammer in Kansas City. David Segui was among the major leaguers who soon adopted his ash bats, but Moyer lost his company in a divorce and moved to Tennessee. He was driving trucks for an insulation firm when company supervisor Chad Lamberth learned of his past and cajoled him back into the business. They began anew in Lamberth's grandmother's garage. They sent a bat to Segui, but this time the first baseman asked if they could make it out of maple. So Old Hickory—named not for the wood used but because it harkens back to

Photo Credit: Old Hickory

Old Hickory, like many of the new bat companies, started small and owed its growth in large part to the explosion of interest in maple bats.

the bats of Babe Ruth—converted to maple and business boomed, prompting one expansion after another. Today they crank out about 40,000 bats per year, nearly three-fourths of which are maple.

Steve McKee worked in printing but saw the writing on the paperless wall of the future and knew it was time to get out of the printing business. He and his two sons, Jeff and Jeremy, had always loved baseball, so the three formed Trinity Bats in Orange County, California. They managed to spread the word quickly through word-of-mouth among major leaguers—Vlad Guerrero was one of the first and he made believers out of his fellow Angels. Then Adrian Gonzalez started ordering bats and his rising star gave business another boost. In 2011 Gonzalez moved from San Diego to Boston. He showed his Trinity bats to new teammate J.D. Drew, who ordered some and who also passed the word on to his brother Stephen in Arizona. "We are at that moment where we have a lot of things in the works," says Jeff McKee. "We are expanding, buying new machines, trying to keep up with the demand. And we are looking at big retail stores next."

Michel Laplante had no intention of becoming a bat manufacturer—the former minor league pitcher had become a manager and pitching coach in his native Quebec, where he also ran a baseball academy. But in 2002 a forest engineer from the area showed up at his office with three logs of yellow birch—Quebec's official tree—saying he and his colleagues believed it would be the ideal wood for a baseball bat. "I kept it in my office but didn't do anything with it," Laplante recalls. "At the end of the season, a friend who was a carpenter made bats out of them and then I was intrigued."

By the following year, Laplante was running the new company B45 Bats (B is for birch, bat, and baseball; the wood comes from the 45th parallel). It may seem an odd job for an ex-pitcher, but Laplante started out as a position player and "always pretended I was a good hitter." He also says he was "fascinated by wood"—he was among the last people he knew using a wooden tennis racket and the only college player he knew using a wooden bat. Laplante is happy that others have followed his lead with birch. "If others help make birch popular, that's good for us and it's good for baseball and good for the Canadian economy," he says. He has chosen to keep his company small, making only 10,000 bats per year and aiming for the high-end market instead of worrying about volume. B45 is also unusual in that it touts its environmental efforts as well—"I hate wasting anything," Laplante says. The company gets its wood from forests certified for sustainable practices; the logs are processed at mills that meet certain environmental standards; all sawdust and wood chips are recovered for use in granular pellets; the bats are produced using hydropower and then painted with natural dyes and varnishes and packaged in highly re-cycled cardboard.

Don Fine's path to the world of bat-making was even more inadvertent. Fine was seeking good wooden bats for his high-school-age son when he dis-covered Split Rock Bats in 2003, then owned by Kevin Kuklis. But Kuklis was also an aspiring pitcher who had a shot at playing winter ball and was ready to shut down the company. Almost on impulse, Fine—unwilling to lose out on the bats his son loved—decided to take over the lathe. He put it in his garage and got some tutoring from Kuklis. Then he expanded operations and built a new workspace behind his house. Finally, he gave up his sales job and devoted himself fully to his bat company, adding Viper Bats and Birch Bats to his line as well. (Producing birch bats also came about accidentally when Fine got a call in 2006 from Rickey Henderson, who wanted some bats. Fine sent him three maples, along with three birch bats he had made as an experiment. After three months without a response, Henderson called and, in his own inimitable style, said, "Rickey likes your bats." But it turned out that without knowing which was which, the Man of Steal had broken the three maple and really liked the birch much better. "The more I used them the more pop they got," Henderson told him, leading Fine into acquiring a new niche for the business.)

Cade Griffis was busy running a baseball academy when he got drawn into the world of wood bats. Griffis started the Dallas Baseball Academy of Texas in 1997, but then a few years later he saw wooden bats coming back into play in local leagues and decided to try making some himself. (He liked wood bats for a variety of reasons, not least of which that his indoor academy was much quieter when players used wood instead of aluminum.) By 2001 D-Bat (an acronym of the academy) was making bats for sale. About four years ago Griffis secured firm contracts with wood suppliers, enabling him to expand, and now D-Bat is cranking out 85,000 bats a year. Even if you've never heard of D-Bat, there's a good chance you've swung one. "We're the largest private label bat-maker in the country," says founder Cade Griffis. "We make bats for 15 other bat companies." With business booming, Griffis is contemplating buying his own mill in the New York-Pennsylvania forests.

The Southern Bat Company is based in the South, the *way* South. Owner Craig Cant went to college in Tennessee, and his twin brother Brett now works in the timber industry in North Carolina. But his Southern Bat Company name goes much further than beyond the Deep South, it goes all the way Down Under. The Cants, who started their company in 2009, hail from Sydney, Australia, where their family once ran a mill for several generations. They claim to be the only company using all Australian timber and labor in their bats. They use Victorian Ash and Tasmanian Oak. "Our goal was to create wood bats for the Australian market at affordable prices," says Craig, whose workshop overlooks the water near his home. He says baseball participation at the amateur level in Australia has been growing rapidly, and in 2010 MLB helped form the Australian Baseball League, giving the sport another boost.

Photo Credit: D-Bat

Between making its own bats and private label bats for 15 other companies, D-Bat keeps itself busy to the tune of 85,000 bats per year.

"I was tired of high priced bats coming from the U.S. being average quality," Cant says, "but it took me a long time to find the right mills with the expertise in finding timber suitable for us at the right price." Currently, the company is only making laminates made over several pieces of wood put together. "This allows us to make sure each bat is consistently heavy enough and strong enough," he explains.

While Craig Cant pursues his labor of love in anonymity on the other side of the globe, Jack Marucci has made a big name for himself in the bigs. Marucci had a perfectly fine career as head athletic trainer of Louisiana State University. Then in 2002 his eight-year-old son Gino decided he wanted a wooden bat. When Marucci couldn't find a suitable one he decided to make one in his backyard tool shed and soon his bats had gone from Lit-

tle Leaguers to major leaguers. First it was Gino's friends and teammates who wanted personalized bats from Marucci's second-hand lathe. Eventually, it was LSU players as well. Marucci formalized a business plan with two LSU alum—and former big leagu-ers—Kurt Ainsworth and Joe Lawrence. He also reached out to Eduardo Perez of the St. Louis Cardinals, who had played at Flori-da State University when Marucci worked there. Marucci persuaded Perez to sample a few bats in 2003.

"I thought, 'Geez, you've got to be kid-ding me,'" Perez later recounted in *Sports Illustrated* when the magazine did a big spread on the rise of Marucci Bats (after a cover photo of Atlanta's hot prospects Jason Heyward and Freddie Freeman, both hefting Marucci bats, served as an indicator of the bat's popularity). "So I humored him with it, and he made me a couple bats. I tried them out at batting practice and thought, 'Wow, these things are really good.'"

Photo Credit: Southern Bat

Craig Cant shows off his Southern Bat Company wares, the only bats made entirely from Australian labor and timber.

Perez helped spread the gospel, first by handing one to a St. Louis team-mate—Albert Pujols. Then he gave one to a former teammate—Barry Lar-kin. With such prominent players giving their implicit endorsement, Perez's word spread and so did the wood. For instance, Pujols initially used them only in batting practice but eventually in games. David Wright—who, along with Jose Reyes, had been sold on the bats by Carlos Beltran, who had gotten into them from Jose Cruz, a former teammate of Perez's—also starting using them. By 2008, Marucci Bats was flourishing enough that the founder bought land in Pennsylvania to get its own wood. Like Akadema, Marucci hired Amish woodcutters.

Even as the company grew, bringing in an outside CEO, it retained its emphasis on quality product. Players spoke glowingly of how Marucci, more than many rivals, only shipped bats that were good enough for game use. (Many players break shipments into three piles—game use, BP, and scrap.) And in the *Sports Illustrated* article, Chase Utley of Philadelphia recalled how before the 2009 World Series, Marucci made a last-minute special order for him—a shorter bat with a larger barrel—just for use against New York's Mariano Rivera. Today, Marucci bats are used by hundreds of major leaguers, and some, like Pujols and Utley, have even invested in the company.

Minor leaguers and even some major leaguers are also swinging Phoenix Bats, but what makes this company special are the bats that no modern professional player would hoist on their shoulder. Phoenix is the leader in the making of 19th-century-style bats.

It all started with the Ohio Village Muffins, a team at the forefront of the burgeoning "vintage" baseball movement in which competitors play by the rules of a specific year, say 1864 or 1884, wearing uniforms and using equipment from that period. Company founder Charles "Lefty" Trudeau played for the Muffins in the early 1990s. He was working in house restoration and had a wood shop, so he started making historically accurate bats for the team, heavier and less tapered than modern sticks. Soon he began researching the original equipment and hand-turning his bats, building his endeavor into a full-fledged business. In 2000 Trudeau formed the Phoenix Bat Company, named for the mythological bird that rises from the ashes, just the way these ancient bats seem to be resurrecting themselves. Ironically, now that it has grown into a full-fledged business, Trudeau uses a computerized lathe to make these old-time bats.

The most popular model of Phoenix Bats is the JT, made in the style of the 1850s-1860s bats, but a bit smaller and better balanced than the biggest sticks from that era. "Players want to recreate the game but still want to play well," Trudeau explains. "If the bat is mammoth, they may not be able to hit the ball." (For those looking for a truly big stick, there are a couple of 37-inch bats, the RB75 and the Mule, in the Phoenix arsenal.)

Phoenix Bats specializes in vintage bats from the early days of baseball, like this replica of a bat used by 19th-century star Cap Anson.

The company is always researching and adding new models, sometimes at a customer's request. For example, someone sent historical notes asking for a well-balanced bat from the 1880s called the Burlingame and it is now a staple of the company. Phoenix has even ventured into the 20th century for a few bats, though some of those are less likely to be used in vintage recreations and more likely to be shown off as souvenirs, like reproductions of Joe Jackson's Black Betsy and the Jackie Robinson-style bat from the 1940s.

Chapter 10

BATS BECOMING BATS
Good wood begins with good wood

> I think that I shall never see
> a poem as lovely as a tree.
>
> *Joyce Kilmer*

All wood bats start off as trees, but it takes a certain kind of tree—often from a very specific location—to create a successful product.

Northern White Ash trees are ideal because of the wood they produce and the way they quickly replenish themselves. About four new trees will grow for every one that gets cut down by the bat-makers. While plenty of maple bats hail from Canada, the vast majority of ash bats used in America today come from one area—the forests along the New York/Pennsylvania border. Go farther north into New England and you encounter those famously harsh winters, which stunt a tree's growth. Such severe weather produces rings too close together and the result is a wood too brittle for baseball bats. To the south, the problem is the opposite—mild winters yield wider rings and wood too soft for bats. But, to quote Goldilocks, the NY/PA border region is just right. (Even here, there are superior spots: The ideal trees for bats are nurtured on the eastern ridge, growing straighter and with less exposure to the summer sun than those on the western slope.)

Hillerich & Bradsby, which chops down about 40,000 trees to make a million bats per year, owns 8,500 acres of land in this area and still buys supplemental timber from other sources. Smaller bat-makers and suppliers ranging from Adirondack (which has its factory in Dolgeville, New York) to many of the newer boutique companies also have bought land in the region.

Foresters spend their days searching for the right trees, ones that usually are 40-60 years old and always at least 16 inches in diameter. The trees selected get chopped down, first with a wedge on the side the tree will topple and then another on the backside. The cutter lodges a metal piece inside to ensure the tree will go in the right direction before giving it one final Ruthian whack. In a nearby clearing, the tree is then cut into 10-to-16-foot chunks, loaded onto trucks, and taken to a mill. A 10-foot log can make 24 bats if the wood is acceptable, but only 10 percent of all logs are made into bats.

The first cuts of wood typically weigh about 20 pounds—and that's to produce a single bat that weighs about two pounds. To make the bat business financially feasible, however, all the wood is used every step of the way. The logs that don't make this first cut are turned into anything from furniture to tool handles; even the sawdust on the floor beneath the lathe at the Louisville Slugger factory winds up being sold off to a turkey farm in Indiana.

At the mill, the best wood will make the next step toward The Show when logs are split into quarters, known as billets. The billets are 40-inch cylinders a little more than three inches in diameter. Long ago, huge stacks of billets would be left out to air dry for months, but today forced-air kilns can do nature's job in a matter of weeks. Then another winnowing-out process takes place—only the billets that have ideal grain lines and no defects will be made into professional bats. When the billets are graded, some are marked for pro bats and others for retail sale or softball, fungo, and toy bats. Then the billets can be cut down to 37 inches and rough-turned to a diameter of 2¾ inches; they weigh from 84-102 ounces, depending on the tree.

The process for maple wood is far more complicated than it is for ash. Put 10,000 ash billets in and 10,000 bats come out, all within an ounce of each other; maple billets must weigh 6.1 to 7.4 pounds, but they must be at exactly the right moisture. Nearly half of the billets turn out too heavy for bat-making. Then each billet must weigh a specific amount to make the bat its appropriate weight. Both of these factors make maple a more labor intensive and costly proposition.

Now it's time to turn this chunk of wood into a bat. Not every bat company follows the exact same process, but the basics are all fairly similar. Bats used to be hand-turned on a lathe—first, one operated by hand crank or foot pedal and then, after 1890, by a steam-powered instrument. This process took 15-30 minutes per bat. But beginning in the 1950s, Hillerich & Bradsby began moving away from the hand-turned bats and letting machines do the work.

While most boutique companies such as Sam Bats still do hand-turning, by the 1990s that step was essentially obsolete for the biggest bat-makers (although they all occasionally tweak a finished bat by hand).

These days, the lathe shaves off the wood and shapes the bat in 30-45 seconds; on the retail side (which also is where bats for minor leaguers are made), H&B's machines, using one of 25 patterns laid into the lathe, crank out 1,000-1,500 bats per day, one after another on the way up the conveyor belt to the sander.

Major league models are done on a computerized lathe that is more precise and consistent than hand-turning and can switch back and forth from one model to another with ease. The computer knows each player's exact preferences; the bats take just under a minute to shape in a process that is mesmerizing to watch. (Louisville Slugger offers public tours of its factory in Louisville.) Although H&B has created more than 2,000 variations on the Louisville Slugger through the years, players today choose from approximately 300 models.

After the bats are shaped, it's on to the belt-sander, which smoothes out the bats, and then it's time for the logo, which is either burned in or, increasingly (especially with bats finished with black, brown, or rose colors), embossed in foil. The trademark goes on the part of the bat called the "flat of the grain"—it is considered the weakest spot in the wood. Players are told to hit *with* the grain (where the bat is strongest) or, putting it another way, with the trademark facing the sky. Yogi Berra paid this tradition no heed, often twisting his bat so he was hitting the ball with the trademark. "I'm up there to hit, not to read," he supposedly said. (In response, Louisville Slugger bat-makers simply shifted the trademark's location on Berra's bats.)

The number in the oval on a Louisville Slugger is the grade of wood, and the lower the better: 125 is the lowest, and it's the number you'll find on major league bats. Just above the oval is the word *Powerized*. In the distant past, it said "Bone Rubbed" because the company marketed the fact that it had adopted the players' old trick for hardening the wood by rubbing a cow bone on the bat and creating a special "bone-rubbed finish." Then the company switched to the word *Powerized* in that spot, accompanied by a bolt of lightning. Up at the barrel is the player's name. Only a select few players who have contracts with the company get their signatures on the bat; the rest have their names

Photo Credit: Louisville Slugger

From forest to factory, from tree to log to billet to bat, the actual process of making bats has not changed much over time, despite the addition of new technologies ranging from trucks to computerized lathes.

printed in block letters. Once burned in, the names are now applied with a laser. (At Rawlings, for the Adirondack bat, the Pro Ring is added to the handle at the end, followed by two coats of lacquer finish.)

The bat is then sanded again, and nubs that had been on each end to help hold the wood during the lathing part of the process are removed. Hillerich & Bradsby used to roll the bat over a live gas flame to burn the grain of the wood slightly, but this Flame Tempering stage, which was simply for aesthetic purposes, is rarely done anymore. The bat subsequently is dipped by machine into the clear or color lacquer finish of the player's choosing before moving on to an infrared oven and cooling unit for about 45 minutes.

Maple bats are made in essentially the same way as ash, but because there's such a variation in density, fewer billets and fewer bats make the final cut, producing more excess wood for furniture, pool cues, Fender Stratocasters, and the like. (One reason for this, Louisville Slugger's master bat-maker Danny Luckett points out, is that with ash, unlike the closed-grained maple, it's possible to spot defects in the billet itself.)

With maple, extra care has to be taken in drying the bats because the wood is more brittle and again in shaping the bats because it is more susceptible to humidity. Because of the more delicate texture, maple bats at Louisville Slugger have a decal laid on instead of being applied with the burning or foil-branding technique. Another major difference is that, while Louisville Slugger makes plenty of maple bats by machine, most of the smaller companies also making maple bats still use hand-turned lathes.

From the end of the World Series through February, bat-makers fill orders for spring training. Some players want their bats sent to the camps, others want them shipped to their homes. (If a player is traded, the order is canceled and then must be rescheduled, because each team has its own bat budget.) But each spring, says Charlotte Jones, who deals with all the big-league teams' equipment managers for Louisville Slugger, there's a mad rush. After Chuck Schupp (the point person for the players) and his staff visit with all teams to find the players' latest preferences, the company cranks out 6,000-7,000 more bats in the four weeks prior to opening day. (Jones points out that a slow season for bat-making no longer exists because the company then begins churning bats—from six standard models—for the minors and top summer collegiate leagues, and by July or August it is fielding orders for the winter leagues.)

Players order even more bats throughout the season and often go through 100 bats in a year. Louisville Slugger gives all starters four free World Series bats (even starting pitchers get two, relievers one). In September 2004, Jones recalls, the Yankees ordered a dozen extra bats for every player on the presumption they'd be playing through the World Series. As it turned out, they had some leftovers after collapsing against the Boston Red Sox in the historic seven-game American League Championship Series that year. The extra lumber, of course, was the least of their wounds.

Chapter 11

ADDING POP TO POP CULTURE
Books, movies, plays, and art featuring bats

But there is no joy in Mudville: Mighty Casey has struck out.

Ernest Lawrence Thayer

One sure sign of the stature of the baseball bat in America, especially compared to gloves or any equipment from other sports, is its favored status in American popular culture.

In poems and novels, on stage and screen, and even in folk and fine art, bats are the subject, the inspiration, and sometimes the raw material. However, Ernest Lawrence Thayer must have dreamed of being a pitcher. How else could baseball's most storied piece of writing have a protagonist—now one of the most famous fictional characters in the history of American letters—stand at the plate with a bat in his hands without once hitting the ball?

Thayer graduated from Harvard in 1885, and his buddy from the *Harvard Lampoon*, William Randolph Hearst, soon hired him to write a humor column for the San Francisco *Examiner*. On June 3, 1888, Thayer's poem "Casey at the Bat" made its debut. With the game on the line, Thayer's batsman plays to the crowd as two strikes shoot past, then the mighty Mudvillian gets serious:

The sneer is gone from Casey's lip, his teeth are clenched in hate;
He pounds with cruel violence his bat upon the plate.
And now the pitcher holds the ball, and now he lets it go,
And now the air is shattered by the force of Casey's blow.

The bat, of course, does no damage to the ball as Casey whiffs…big time. "Casey at the Bat," originally published under Thayer's nickname Phin, could easily have vanished without a trace. But it was partially excerpted in the New

York *Sun*, and a New York man named Archibald Gunter liked it so much he clipped it out. Several weeks later, Gunter's friend, the comic performer De Wolf Hopper, learned that the New York Giants and Chicago White Stockings were coming to see his opera company perform *Prince Methusalem* and he really wanted to present a baseball bit in tribute to this special audience.

Voila! Gunter produced the poem. At Wallack's Theatre in New York on August 14, 1888, the deep-voiced Hopper gave a highly dramatic reading of "Casey at the Bat" and "the audience literally went wild," the New York *World* proclaimed.

The *Sun* had not named an author when it ran its excerpted version of "Casey at the Bat," so no one knew who wrote it. In fact authorship was a matter of dispute for years before Thayer received full acclaim. Apparently a dismal performer of his own work, Thayer owes some debt to Hopper for popularizing it. Hopper gave his 5-minute, 40-second reading about 10,000 times in the next decade. (That performance now feels dated and mannered; for a performance with a more modern—yet still suitably over-the-top—dramatic flourish, search online for James Earl Jones' reading of the poem.)

The inspiration for Casey is believed by some to be Boston star Mike "King" Kelly, whom Thayer had seen play at Harvard and while covering games for the *Examiner*. Thayer denied such a connection, saying he based the poem upon a high school bully named Daniel Casey. (Kelly performed Casey on the vaudeville circuit. He changed the character to "Mighty Kelly"—an odd choice, given the batter's performance—and that switch no doubt did not sit well with Thayer.) No matter what, however, Casey

DE WOLF HOPPER

Photo Credit: Library of Congress

"Casey at the Bat" might have been quickly forgotten had it not fallen into the hands of comic performer De Wolf Hopper, who made it famous with 10,000 public performances over a decade.

has been recited, revised and republished countless times and in countless forms since its publication. Garrison Keillor tells the story from the perspective of the opposing team's fans; Hart Seely and Frank Cammuso imagine what it would have been like if the inning had been announced with the meandering digressions of the late New York Yankee broadcaster Phil Rizzuto; and *Mad Magazine* has returned to the material numerous times, including one in which Casey is a free agent and one called "Barry at the Bat," about Barry Bonds and his steroid scandal. There are dozens of variations collected in *The Annotated Casey at the Bat*. In some he hits a home run, in others his wife or daughter strikes out, in a modern rendition he ends up in arbitration; one raunchy version called "Casey on the Bat" even plays off the obscure use of the word *bat* as another way of saying *prostitute*.

Casey may have struck out, but Thayer had hit a mighty home run. And while he was among the first to draw upon the game for inspiration, baseball has always held a unique place in the American heart, and writers and filmmakers have eternally tried capturing that connection.

The love affair with the baseball bat itself begins in childhood—what kid doesn't at least briefly feel bigger, stronger, more powerful and capable when wielding a bat—and many children's books deal not only with the sport but with the idea of becoming the big hitter. Cartoonist Charles Schulz, of course, took a different and unique path. "Peanuts" often dealt with baseball and, while its most iconic images are of

Photo Credit: Library of Congress, LC-USZC2-6148

Charles Schulz was a passionate baseball fan and imbued his love of the game into his most lovable creation, Charlie Brown.

those hapless kids (and one dog) in the field yielding run after run, when the Peanuts gang did finally get up to the plate, poor ol' Charlie Brown continued suffering new indignities…even when it wasn't his turn to bat. In one sequence he advises the next batter, "Keep the trademark up Lucy, and there'll be less chance of cracking the bat," only to have Lucy hold the bat with the trademark up as she watches three strikes zip by; she returns to the bench and blithely says, "You were right, manager…I kept the trademark up and I didn't crack the bat," prompting a distressed Charlie Brown to moan, "My stomach hurts."

Even when Charlie Brown finally hits not one but two game-winning home runs in 1993, things don't go according to plan. After the first game, the losing pitcher, Royanne Hobbs, tells Charlie Brown, "you ruined my life," but after the second time she declares she let him win on purpose because she felt sorry for him. Hobbs also claims after the first game to be the granddaughter of Roy Hobbs, the protagonist of *The Natural* and is undeterred when Charlie Brown tells her that Hobbs was a fictional character. Royanne even manages to con Lucy into buying what Royanne promises is Roy Hobbs' bat. When Lucy learns she has been duped, she lashes out at Royanne, a character who soon disappeared from "Peanuts" altogether.

Among the traditional stories that revolved around bats, the most successful was *The Lucky Baseball Bat*, the first children's book ever published by Matt Christopher (in 1954), who spent the next forty years as the most prolific children's sports author in the country. (Even since his death there are still Matt Christopher books being published, penned by other authors under his name.) His debut novel tells the tale of the new kid in town, Martin, who struggles to make friends on the baseball team until a teenager gives him his old bat. With this new lumber Martin can't miss and becomes a star. But then the bat goes missing and Martin must learn that it was really him and his newfound confidence—and not the bat—that was responsible for his success. The baseball scenes in this children's classic are captivating, and many kids, who are almost as superstitious as professional ballplayers, can relate to Martin's angst.

While most children's baseball books chart a similar path, there a few more original voices out there, like Gavin Curtis' *The Bat Boy and the Violin*. In this memorable story about life in the Negro Leagues after Jackie Robinson integrated baseball, a violin-playing boy named Reginald is pressed into service as the batboy by his father, manager of the league's worst team. Reginald's dad hopes to make the boy more manly, but his son is a total oaf when it comes to handling the bats; he is, however, a major league talent on the violin, and the team rallies to the sound of his music and his father finally comes to appreciate Reginald for who he is.

Grown-ups get their share of baseball stories too, of course, but when it comes to the bat itself, one story casts the longest shadow. The most famous fictional bat belonged to Roy Hobbs, the protagonist of *The Natural*, which in its original form was far from a pastoral tale about our national pastime. Bernard Malamud's novel was a dark rumination on American greed. But most people only know the movie version of Hobbs, as portrayed by the All-American hero Robert Redford. The 1984 film plays better for families than the novel would, although it is as over-the-top and unbelievably sappy in its happy ending as Malamud's 1952 novel was overwritten and heavy-handed in its dark allegory.

Photo Credit: National Baseball Hall of Fame

The most famous fictional bat in baseball history, Wonderboy, was crafted by Roy Hobbs from a tree struck by lightning. In the end of the movie version, however, Hobbs achieves lasting glory with a different bat, named the Savoy Special.

Still, the story of Hobbs resonates in large part not because of his climactic final game but because of the lifelong love affair with his own handmade bat: Wonderboy.

"I made it long ago, when I was a kid," Hobbs explained in the book and in similar words in the movie. "I wanted it to be a very good bat, and that's why I gave it that name…. This tree near the river where I lived was split by lightning. I liked the wood inside of it, so I cut me out a bat…. I wanted it to be special."

The movie shows the lightning dramatically striking the tree, then a pair of hands lovingly crafting the bat and burning the name Wonderboy and a lightning bolt into the barrel. Wherever he went, Hobbs carried the bat in a special case—a bassoon case in the book, a trombone case in the movie.

After Hobbs' promising career is derailed in his youth by a violent encounter with a femme fatale, he emerges seemingly from nowhere in his mid-30s to earn a shot with the New York Knights. Manager Pop Fisher ignores him as long as he can, but when Hobbs finally gets a chance to take batting practice and puts on a mind-boggling show, the skipper calls the slugger over and demands, "Let me see that bat."

"Sure is white," Pop says. "Did you bleach the wood?" Told "no, that's the true color," the manager then instructs his coach to measure and weigh the bat. "If it comes up to specifications," Pop allows, "we'll let you use it." (This a gaffe by Malamud. There is no maximum weight for a bat, and anyone could easily eyeball a bat and know whether it exceeds the legal 42 inches. The movie lays it on thick, with a newsreel showing the bat meeting official standards.) In the film, Hobbs' teammates study and admire Wonderboy, with one saying in awe, "There's not a mark on it, not a nick," which Hobbs explains by saying, "I boned it so it wouldn't chip." (This is also pure fantasy. All wooden bats chip eventually.)

In the big game at the end of the film, lightning flashes in the sky and then Hobbs breaks his special bat on a foul ball. Roy is momentarily distraught, but he soon turns to the eager batboy, Bobby Savoy, and says, "Go pick me out a winner." The kid comes back with a homemade bat of his own called the "Savoy Special." After Hobbs exchanges a special smile with the lad, he returns to the plate and, with blood from an injury seeping through his jersey, blasts a home run into the light fixtures, which explode alongside fireworks that are accompanied by swelling Hollywood music. The book goes just as far to the opposite end of the spectrum, with Hobbs breaking his bat and striking out. Unable to bear seeing Wonderboy in pieces, he ties it together with his shoelaces, buries it in the ground and wishes "it would take root and become a tree."

In a brilliant parody, Homer J. Simpson—an equally beloved and perhaps more truly representative American icon than Robert Redford—wielded his own "secret weapon": Wonder Bat. "It all started last year during a terrible thunderstorm, when I locked myself out of the house," Homer explains to Bart in an episode of "The Simpsons" called "Homer at the Bat." "Sheltering myself with a large piece of sheet metal, I ran for cover under the tallest tree I could find! A bolt of lightning struck the tree, and a branch fell down. Something told me this was a very special, very magical, piece of wood that I could make a bat out of."

So Homer puts aside his efforts to create a homemade football and carves himself Wonder Bat, which he keeps in a special case. He goes on a home run spree that propels the Springfield Zephyrs, made up of guys from the local nuclear power plant, to the brink of softball greatness (and inspires his teammates to get their own special bats, though they grab things like a piano leg or a sister's prosthetic limb). Then the evil and greedy Mr. Burns bets a million dollars on the championship game against Shelbyville and hires ringers like Wade Boggs, Roger Clemens, Jose Canseco, Ozzie Smith, and Darryl Strawberry to play for the Zephyrs. In practice before the game, Wonder Bat is shattered by one flaming Clemens' fastball. And even when most of the major leaguers are felled by various means (Wade Boggs is knocked out by the drunken Barney in a debate about the greatest prime minister in British history, for example), Strawberry is still there to play right field, Homer's position. But in the ninth inning with the game tied at 43-43, two outs, and the bases loaded, Mr. Burns, playing the percentages, calls on right-handed Homer to pinch hit for the left-handed Strawberry against a southpaw (despite Strawberry's nine home runs in the game). Grabbing a bat off the ground, Homer goes to the plate. But he never gets to swing because he gets beaned on the first pitch, knocking home the winning run by being knocked unconscious.

Unlike *The Natural*, the best baseball movies tend to be cheerfully profane and as concerned with the poetry of the game and its characters as with the final outcome. In *Bull Durham*, a hopeful batboy urges veteran catcher Crash Davis (Kevin Costner) to get a hit. Crash snaps "shut up," then strikes out. One struggling hitter in the movie, Jose, has a "chicken-bone cross" that he uses to take the curse off his bat; another hitter, in a 0-for-16 skid and on the verge of being let go, begs to touch it but Jose says only true believers, not the merely desperate, can benefit from it. Then Crash undoes all that by sneaking a touch on the sly and going out and hitting his first homer of the season.

But the most famous voodoo batter in Hollywood baseballdom is Pedro

Cerrano in the movie *Major League*. Played by Dennis Haysbert years before his role as President David Palmer on the TV series "24," Cerrano builds a shrine for his bats, telling perplexed teammates that the bats "are sick" and that's why he can't hit a curveball. "I ask Jobu to come, take fear from bats," Cerrano explains. "I offer him cigar, rum."

Later, when a born-again player is imposing his prayers on the entire team, Cerrano, trying to wake up his bats, explodes his incense and sets off the clubhouse sprinkler system. Cerrano's most famous line comes when he appropriates his teammate's golf club covers: "Hats for bats," he says appreciatively. "Keep bats warm. Gracias."

Finally, just like the boy in *The Lucky Baseball Bat*, Pedro learns he needs to believe only in himself. In the big playoff game, he blasts a crucial home run, kisses his bat, and carries it around the bases.

Given the central role of baseball in the American cultural landscape, it's no surprise that the bat has long been a symbol of strength and power. It is so potent that it often extends beyond the diamond and into the field of law and order. One tough guy who forged a connection between baseball and Hollywood was Buford Pusser, a former wrestler who became a Tennessee legend in the 1960s by taking on moonshiners and murderers, often armed with only a large wooden club or a baseball bat. He was celebrated in *Walking Tall*, a 1973 film starring Joe Don Baker, although on film Pusser usually pinch-hit for his bat with a hand-carved wooden bludgeon. This image of a bat-wielding lawman was parodied on the 1970s television satire "Soap," when Burt Campbell ran for sheriff, got ambushed by the forces of corruption, used a bat as a weapon, and gained fame as Sheriff "Bat" Campbell (a nod to real-life western lawman William "Bat" Masterson).

While bats do show up in movies in non-weapon roles—in *A Few Good Men* Lt. Daniel Kaffee (played by Tom Cruise) always holds a bat and when he can't find it moans, "I need my bat. I think better with my bat"—most frequently it seems Hollywood directors seem to think that bats are made for bashing.

Perhaps moviemakers have spent too much time listening to music, where songs involving baseball bats almost invariably involve violence. Most famous is the classic Ramones punk anthem, "Beat on the Brats," with its chorus, "Beat on the brats with the baseball bats." (The Ramones' record label tried promoting the song with mini-Louisville Slugger plastic bats but a threatened lawsuit forced them to strip the bat-maker's name off.) But every genre from rock (Goo Goo Dolls) to punk (The Have Nots) to hip-hop (Eazy E) to country (Carrie Underwood) features songs where baseball bats are smashing people or car headlights, not baseballs. (There are a few notable exceptions like Kenny Rogers' tender and wry "The Greatest" and Dire Straits' "The Bug," which philosophically notes, "Sometimes you're the Louisville Slugger, sometimes you're the ball.")

Whatever the motivation, screenwriters and directors have created a long parade of heavy hitters in movies:

- *The Apostle:* Sonny Dewey (played by Robert Duvall) finds his wife having an affair and beats the other man senseless.

- *Falling Down:* frustrated and downsized Bill "D-Fens" Foster (played by Michael Douglas) is unable to complete his Los Angeles commute because he doesn't have correct change; when a Korean store clerk refuses to give him change, Foster grabs the clerk's sawed-off bat and trashes the store with it. (Later Foster beats up a couple of thugs with it before really arming himself with guns and howitzers.)

- *The Principal:* Rick Latimer (played by Jim Belushi) takes over the world's toughest school and uses a bat as a prop; later he's being held at knife point when one of his students saves him by swatting the bad guy with the bat. This may have been inspired by the more realistic but less violent story of *Lean On Me*, which told of Joe Clark (played by Morgan Freeman), a principal at a rough school in Paterson, New Jersey. Clark gained notoriety in the 1980s when he brought the student body under control by walking the halls with a Louisville Slugger in hand.

- *Warriors:* a Brooklyn street gang named the Warriors gets attacked by every other gang in the city, including the Baseball Furies, who dress in baseball uniforms, paint their faces, and wield bats…which the Warriors take away from them and then use themselves…with a fury.

- *Escape from New York:* John Carpenter's 1980s cult classic features a battle to the death at a ruined Madison Square Garden between Snake Plissken (played by Kurt Russell) and a humungous henchman of the evil Duke. While everyone thought Snake would lose, he survives the fight by swinging a nail-studded bat with great force. (Unlike many movie stars who lack the athletic ability to really swing a bat, Russell had been a solid hitter in the low minor leagues before a rotator cuff injury and his burgeoning Hollywood career ended his diamond days.)

- *Signs:* M. Night Shyamlan's alien-invasion flick features a failed minor leaguer slugger Merrill Hess (played by Joaquin Phoenix). When an alien invades the family home and takes a captive, he's encouraged to save the day by his father (played by a surprisingly calm Mel Gibson), who urges him to take a bat—which Merrill had used to hit a 507-foot homer—off the wall and "swing away." Merrill makes solid contact.

- *Zombieland:* Tallahassee (played by Woody Harrelson) uses an aluminum bat with a donut still on it to take out a zombie with one perfect swing. (Of course, the movie then goes over the top with a gratuitous bashing shot.)

- *Casino:* Mob movies have always loved a good bat beating, even acknowledging it in a parody like *The Crew*, which featured Burt Reynolds as a character named Joey Bats. But one of the most horrific uses of a bat in a movie was the relentlessly violent realism in *Casino*, where Nicky Santoro (played by Joe Pesci) and his brother are both beaten nearly to death in a cornfield by mobsters wielding aluminum bats. (The two are then stripped and buried alive.)

- *Office Space:* The *Casino* beating was so memorable that director Mike Judge parodied it in his workplace comedy, with the office dweebs administering the beating to a printer instead of a person. At the 10th-anniversary reunion the cast were all given bats and reenacted this beloved moment (which has also inspired numerous YouTube copycats).

- *Naked Gun: From the Files of Police Squad:* Mike Judge wasn't the first to find the laughs in bat violence. The set-up for this movie's beloved baseball scene comes when Lieutenant Frank Drebin (played by Leslie Nielsen) asks an umpire "Is this an official bat?" and then knocks the ump out with one swing and takes over his job in an effort to thwart a crime. (During the on-field shenanigans, Drebin searches for weapons everywhere and checks one bat with a corkscrew, a nod to real hitters' propensity for corking their bats.)

- *50 First Dates:* This movie not only plays a bat beating for laughs, it even lets a woman inflict the crazed violence. Enhancing the viewers' enjoyment is the fact that the cheerful Drew Barrymore is pummeling the obnoxious Rob Schneider.

If, however, there ever is to be an Oscar for Best Use of Baseball Bat to Violent Ends, the nominees would have to be:

- *The Shining:* Perhaps there's no one who can be more menacing on screen than Jack Nicholson, especially here, when he's playing a possessed Stephen King character. When his character, Jack Torrance, finally becomes completely unglued in the isolated Overlook Hotel, his wife Wendy (played by Shelly Duvall) tries keeping him at bay with a bat. She chokes up way too much, however, and seems utterly ineffectual swinging weakly while backing away as he threatens her, "I'm not going to hurt you Wendy, I'm going to bash your head right in" and then sneers that she should "give me the bat." Finally she does give it to him, connecting with one good shot that topples him down a flight of stairs and sets the climactic scenes in motion.

- *The Untouchables:* When we first meet Al Capone (played by Robert DeNiro), he's presenting a likable face as he charms the press. In the first 40 minutes of the movie there is not even a hint of violence from him. Capone has relatively little screen time in the movie, so he must establish his presence with bold strokes. And, as chillingly played by DeNiro, he does so while seething with anger over Elliot Ness' first successful raid. At a black tie dinner with his mob cohorts, he goes on about Ness' "enthusiasms" before eliciting chuckles all around by saying that his own "enthusiasm" is for baseball. He gives a long speech, with bat in hand, about how a batter enjoys the chance for individual achievement but must also play the field as part of a team. (Capone obviously had to contend with Ness and other government agents but never with the designated hitter!) This elicits murmurs of good-natured approval, until Capone takes out the weak link on his team—the man whose stash was raided—with a hard, crushing thonk, smashing his bat into the man's head. As the victim falls face first onto the dinner table Capone savagely beats him three more times. Blood spills forth and the true Capone is finally revealed.

- *Inglorious Basterds:* In *The Shining* and *The Untouchables*, it is the legendary Hollywood stars that give the bat scenes such heft. But *Inglorious Basterds* is all about the twisted genius of director Quentin Tarantino. The scene with the bat-wielding Bear Jew is no exception. This outrageous revisionist history features a group of American soldiers hunting Nazi scalps during World War II. In one of the most famous scenes, the leader Aldo Raine (played by Brad Pitt) munches on a sandwich in the forest while an uncooperative Nazi prisoner kneels, listening to a banging sound that is emanating from a tunnel and growing closer and closer. Soon he, and the audience, learns the sound was Donnie Donowitz (played by Eli Roth), the maniacal Bear Jew, hitting his bat against the tunnel wall. Donowitz, who hails from Boston, then bashes in the prisoner's head and gleefully shouts like a broadcaster after a home run that "Teddy Ballgame" has really connected. The scene was even memorialized in a movie poster and

DVD cover, with a Nazi helmet dangling from a bloody and dented bat. (Instead of Louisville, Kentucky, in the bat's logo, Tarantino wrote Knoxville, Tennessee, a nod to his hometown.)

- *Do the Right Thing*: Sal (played by Danny Aiello), is the one hardworking, honest, and fair man in Spike Lee's complex and controversial masterpiece. The longtime owner of a pizza joint in Brooklyn's Bedford-Stuyvesant neighborhood, he must balance his racist son Pino (played by John Turturro), his irresponsible delivery boy Mookie (played by Spike Lee himself), and the intermittently hostile behavior of his mostly black customers. But when Radio Raheem (played by Bill Nunn) purposely antagonizes him by breaking the pizzeria rules with his obnoxiously loud boom-box for the second time in one very hot, very long day, Sal finally loses his cool. He grabs the baseball bat he keeps for protection and "kills" the boom box in a barrage of blows. As violence begets ever worse violence we see the bat, in a way, as the match that sets the blaze in this movie's incendiary finale.

This Oscar category may be imaginary but there is one actual Tony Award winner that features a baseball bat in a crucial supporting role. August Wilson's *Fences*, which won for Best Play in 1987 and Best Revival in 2010, tells the story of an embittered Negro Leaguer Troy Maxson and the fences that can't keep his family and his world together. One of the most critical scenes is a fight between a drunk Troy and his teenage son Cory, who has come to resent his father's angry, domineering ways. In the scene, Cory grabs the baseball bat Troy always keeps in the yard to swing at a piece of rag tied to a tree. But Cory is unable to use it against his father, who grabs the weapon and turns it on his son. Yet after driving Cory from his home, Maxson remains trapped in his own world; we later find out that he dies from a heart attack in the yard while swinging the bat that symbolized to him the devastating price of racism and segregation.

In recent years baseball bats also have become an increasingly popular motif in folk and fine art worlds. While the sport has long served as a muse for folk artists, like the anonymous craftsman who carved a wooden hitter then gave him an oversized metal whisk with which to slug the ball, it has moved into previously unimagined realms.(There are also crafts people re-imagining broken or old bats in new ways, as salt shakers, table legs, and even wedding rings.)

In 1998 a human-rights-themed art exhibition displayed a highly unusual political piece by a Pittsburgh-based artist named Andrew Johnson called "Choke: Witness for Peace." The work was a 34-inch baseball bat painted a flesh-color and covered with what appears to about four-dozen real animal eyes. Johnson apparently used a baseball bat because of reports of a bat found in a torture chamber in Kosovo that was labeled "mouth-shutter" and added the eyes to show how even human rights advocates can fail to see things clearly and can be hypocritical when it comes to bludgeoning (albeit metaphorically) their opponents on certain issues.

In 2001 artist Alison Saar carved heads into the barrels of eight darkly stained bats, then isolated them in a corner of the room when they were on display as "Bat Boyz," a tribute to the men who endured the isolation of playing baseball before integration.

Photo Credit: Louisville Slugger Museum & Factory

The Hillerich & Bradsby office is home to several whimsical bat-related artworks, including "Infield Fly," a bat with a zipper on it.

Plenty of artists stick more closely to the traditional and lighter themes and, not surprisingly, the Hillerich & Bradsby office is home to some of the more memorable pieces. There is the whimsical "Infield Fly" (a bat with a zipper on it), the delicate "Soul of the Game" (a bat with its outer skin removed that looks hollow underneath), and in president Jack Hillerich's office a rocking chair made of bats and a table shaped like a bat.

Most of these works are tucked away for private enjoyment. At the opposite end of the spectrum are public works of art, many of which are not only grander in scale but are also often more whimsical or concerned with the aesthetic beauty of the bat itself. Perhaps the most famous is in Chicago, where in 1977 pop artist Claes Oldenburg installed "Batcolumn" in front of a government building—the steel sculpture, which is about 100-feet tall and weighs about 20-tons, echoes the architectural columns of a nearby train station while also forcing people to rethink their impression of everyday objects. Oldenburg called it a monument to "baseball and to the construction industry...a celebration of steel construction as well as to the ambition and vigor Chicago likes to see in itself."

Many objected to the idea of paying taxpayer dollars for what was deemed blatantly unimaginative—the Chicago *Tribune's* architecture critic slammed "Batcolumn" as ludicrous, and when it first debuted a drunk told a reporter, "Give me a dollar and I could build something better than that." But in the end, it has become a Chicago landmark.

Seattle's Safeco Field, by contrast, is a place where sports-themed art makes sense. Swinging and swirling down from the atrium ceiling is Linda Beaumont's "The Tempest," a tremendous chandelier/sculpture of 1,500 bats along an aluminum frame. The Seattle *Times* art critic called it "very likely the most remarkable piece of public art ever installed in a sports facility."

In the summer of 2003, the entire city of Cincinnati—the birthplace of professional baseball—went batty for baseball art. A local group called ArtWorks created Bats Incredible!, a public art initiative that brought to the city's streets, plazas, hotels, and office lobbies nearly 200 sculptures built from a total of 11,000 regulation Louisville Sluggers. (An estimated one million people saw the works; most pieces were auctioned off after several months on display.)

Among the highlights:

- "Just for the HaliBat," by Carus Waggoner, was a 15-foot-tall, 12-foot-long fish skeleton, with a fiberglass and foam head, oversized Christ-

Photo Credit: Ben VanHouten

Linda Beaumont's "The Tempest" is a tremendous chandelier/sculpture of 1,500 bats along an aluminum frame swirling down from the ceiling at Seattle's Safeco Field.

mas ornaments for eyes, and the skeleton made of bats. (Waggoner originally planned a different creature—"The LouisvilleSlug"—but too many people were grossed out by the idea.)

- "Batum Dunn," designed by Michael Schuster, was a 10-feet-high, 12-feet-long, 2,500 pound sculpture of a lefty slugger (like then Reds' star Adam Dunn) swinging at a pitch, but his bones were a stainless steel frame and his rippling muscles were 78 bats. A similar project by Jon Hand was "Kneeds to Play" which featured a batter made of 50 bats poised in a Pete Rose-inspired stance.

- "Batzilla," by Steve Brauch, used 100 bats (along with fiberglass, foam, and plenty of green paint) to create a bat-built tribute to the famous Japanese monster. (Brauch also contributed "Bats in the Belfry," a bell made entirely of bats.)

- "One Swingular Sensation," created by sculptor Stephanie Cooper with students at the Ursula Academy, paid homage to the Broadway musical *A Chorus Line* by using 72 brightly painted bats to make a kick line of 12 pairs of dancing legs.

- *Johnny's Bench*, by Frank Stanton, was a simple but clever concept—a bench made entirely of bats with a picture of the Reds' Hall of Fame catcher adorning it.

- "Sparky Rodinderson: The Pinch-Thinker," was a bat-built sculpture that is an homage to Rodin's famous

Photo Credit: ?

"Johnny's Bench" is simple but clever—a bench made entirely of bats with a picture of the Reds' Hall of Fame catcher adorning it.

sculpture "The Thinker." The artist, Joel Selmeier, also had an American flag made out of painted bats called "Batsy Ross." On his own website (www.joel.com), Selmeier went even further, developing virtual sculptures for everything from "Robats," a kinetic piece, to parking meters constructed with bats, to "Leaning Tower of Bats" and "Batful Tower," to an homage to world-renowned blown-glass artist Dale Chihuly.

In 2006 the American Association of Woodturners devoted their annual traveling exhibition to baseball with a show called "Step Up to the Plate." Fittingly, it debuted at the Louisville Slugger Museum and featured a wide array of wood pieces, many naturally revolving around bats: J. Paul Fennel's "Wood-turner's Wiffleball & Wifflebat" has a delicate-looking hollow 30" maple bat with intricate patterns on the hole-filled surface; Bonnie Klein's "One Black

Bat for Junior" is an ivorywood and African blackwood necklace featuring 41 miniature bats, only one of which is black, in honor of Ken Griffey Jr.'s stick; William Smith's "Answer to the Screwball," which has maple and walnut stripes twisting the length of the bat; and Jack Rogers' "WOW!!! That was a fast one" includes a bat, the "Louisville Whacker," with a hole burned out in the barrel as if a fastball just blazed right through it.

Perhaps the league leader—bat-wise—from the Woodturners show was Mark Sfirri, who contributed pieces from his "Rejects from the Bat Factory" series. "Inch Worm bat" is a maple bat that looks like an inchworm in mid-crawl, "Stubbed" is a bat that seems to have crashed into home plate and bent itself in the process, and his collaboration with Jacques Vesery, "It Boils Down to This," is a rough-surfaced bat with a sugar maple spout attached. Another of his Rejects is the "Exotics" collection, which features an assortment of playfully deformed bats

Photo Credit: Mark Sfirri

These playfully deformed bats from Mark Sfirri's series, "Rejects from the Bat Factory" are made from exotic woods like cocobolo and zebrawood.

made from exotic woods like zebrawood and cocobolo. One untitled piece that wasn't in the show, which Sfirri made just for fun, is a five-foot-long bat he made while the wood was still green and then steam dried to create a bend in it.

Another definite highlight of the bats displayed was Alan Stirt's "Enhanced Bat," which imagines what a bat would look like on steroids—it is a Stan Olozol model, a mocking tribute to Stanolozol, a popular steroid.

But perhaps no one is more committed to the intersection of baseball bats and art than Gary Mifflin (www.baseballbatart.com). Mifflin is a woodworker and custom-stair builder who got started in this field when he decided to make a bat for his son to use in a game. Making his son's bat started him thinking not only about how the shape hasn't basically changed at all in decades but also about how players taper handles and add their own unique touches. "I started wondering what else you can do to a bat. I'm a baseball fan, a woodworker, and an artist, so I started going crazy."

Photo Credit: Gary Mifflin

In Gary Mifflin's "Pressure" (made of ash and walnut), a bat has collapsed into itself.

Only two of Mifflin's sculptures actually use bats, most notably "Louie," an old-time baseball player made out of a Louisville Slugger. His other works are baseball-themed sculptures with the "bats" made of different woods. In "Fastball" (made of red leaf maple), a ball has split the bat and become embedded in it; in "Pressure" (ash and walnut), a bat has collapsed into itself; "Abandoned Veteran" (ash) is a wilted old-timer; "Tied Up" (ash) plays off the cliché about a pitcher getting a hitter tied up in knots; and the melted bat of "August Heat" (red leaf maple) is a tribute to the oppressive summers at the ballpark in his hometown of St. Louis.

Mifflin has created a company to sell versions of his signature piece, "The Arch," a depiction of St. Louis' Gateway Arch as if it were made from a bat. But since he has a day job that pays his bills, Mifflin has decided he doesn't want to sell his other works individually, though he has had them displayed together. "I think they're most interesting as a group," he says. And it's a group that keeps growing. "I've got a lot of other drawings already. Now I'm obsessed with bats."

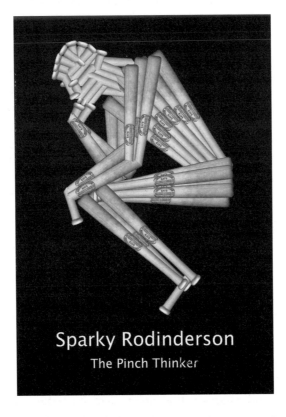

Sparky Rodinderson

The Pinch Thinker

"Sparky Rodinderson: The Pinch Thinker" is Joel Selmeier's bat-built sculptural homage to Rodin's famous "The Thinker."

Chapter 12

THE MVB AWARD
The most valuable bat of all time?

Ladies and gentlemen, I just want to say one thing.
I am proud I hit the first home run here, against Boston in 1923.

Babe Ruth, weeks before his death in 1948,
on his last visit to Yankee Stadium
in celebration of the 25ᵗʰ anniversary of the "House Ruth Built"

Since America is a nation of consumers and collectors it is impossible to write a book about baseball bats without touching on the idea of bats as commerce.

It would be naïve to wish that baseball's most historic moments and iconic players would be treasured simply for what or who they were, and we are a nation of consumers and collectors. And so it should not be surprising that a society that can create a market for a million dollar baseball card would put a pretty high price on the most coveted game-used bats from baseball history. On the bright side, however, the market has generally proven a fairly astute judge of baseball greatness. So it should also be equally unsurprising that the real MVB—Most Valuable Bat—belonged to Babe Ruth.

Before the first game ever played in the "new" Yankee Stadium in 1923, Ruth proclaimed "I'd give a year of my life if I can hit a home run in the first game in this new park." That dramatic declaration was driven by several factors. Ruth knew he was essentially the sole reason for the Yankees building their grand new ballpark. But he also knew how far he had fallen in the eyes of the public since the construction had begun. After revolutionizing baseball by blasting hitting 54 homers in 1920 and 59 in 1921, after leading the Yankees to their first ever pennant, after becoming one of the nation's most prominent and adored celebrities, Ruth had come up injured in the 1921 World Series against the New York Giants as the Yankees lost. Ruth then earned numerous suspensions in 1922 for everything from barnstorming to throwing dirt at an

Babe Ruth remains perhaps baseball's greatest hero—even this bat from his pitching days in Boston sold for $537,750, making it the third most expensive bat ever.

ump to charging a heckler. He managed only 35 homers that year, failing to lead the league, and then suffered through a 2-17 effort in the World Series as the Yankees again lost to John McGraw's Giants. Finally, Ruth had faced (false) rape charges and subsequently struggled during spring training in 1923.

But when Opening Day finally arrived, on April 18, 1923, Ruth erased all that turmoil with a single stroke, smashing a three-run homer in the third inning, propelling the Yankees to a 4-1 victory—against the very Boston team that had self-destructed years earlier by selling him to New York.

Ruth donated the 36-inch, 45½-ounce Louisville Slugger he used to slug his home run to the Los Angeles *Evening Herald*, which gave it to a local 16-year-old named Victor Orsatti, named the area's top high-school slugger. Ruth inscribed the bat "To the Boy Home Run King of Los Angeles;" Orsatti kept it until his death in 1984 when he willed it to his caretaker, Marcia Napoli-Tejada, who kept it under her bed for twenty years before finally selling it off at auction.

In 1998 the ball Ruth blasted in that first game was sold for a then-record $126,500; meanwhile, the bat he used in his final game at Yankee Stadium had gone for $107,000, while a bat he used in his final game ever went for $74,000. But when the 1923 bat, dubbed "the Sultan of Swag" finally came on the market, it was auctioned off for $1.27 million by Sotheby's in 2004.

The Ruth bat was just the third piece of baseball memorabilia to break the million-dollar barrier (besides a rare Honus Wagner baseball card and Mark McGwire's 70th home run ball, which has probably lost much of its value after McGwire's steroids confessions and Barry Bonds' 73-home run season). Fittingly, given Ruth's early childhood when he was shipped off away from home to an institution for troubled boys, Napoli-Tejada announced she was donating a portion of her proceeds to an orphanage.

Since then, a bat Ruth used in 1918 when he helped the Boston Red Sox win the World Series was auctioned for $537,750 to become the third most expensive bat ever, even though he was still primarily a pitcher at that point. A bat he used to bash his then-record 58th and 59th homers in 1921 sold for $483,000 in 2006, and a 1924 Ruth bat went for $195,000 in 2008. (Three other Ruth bats that sold before 2001 are also in the game's top 10, reaping $150,000-$320,000 each.)

Before Ruth came along, Joe Jackson was among the greatest hitters of the deadball era. So it is not inappropriate that before Ruth's bat shattered all marks, Jackson held the record for the highest price ever hit by a bat at auction. Of course, it's worth noting the irony that Jackson's bat sold on eBay in 2001 for $577,610, a sum more than 100 times the amount he was given in the Black Sox Scandal that ended his career and forever stained his name. Of course, that is one reason why the bat was worth so much. (To cash in on the interest stirred up by the auction, Louisville Slugger even made 500 limited edition replicas, retailing for $150 each.)

In August 2011 the bat was sold again, this time for $537,750 with Heritage Auction's touting it once again as the "original Black Betsy." But while Jackson's Black Betsy may be among the most famous bats in the game, there is legitimate reason to question whether this is indeed that bat.

The bat was auctioned off the first time by Lester Erwin (called Lester Ervin on the Heritage Auctions website), the son of a cousin of Jackson's widow Kate. He had been only five years old when Jackson died and thirteen when Kate died, bequeathing it to him. (She simply willed him a bat, never calling it

Photo Credit: Heritage Auctions

Though it seems unlikely that this was the original Black Betsy, it was clearly a favorite of Joe Jackson and has the famous unique bend in the handle.

Black Betsy.) The bludgeon clearly traced its roots back a long way. The question is how long.

According to lore, Charlie Ferguson, a woodworker in his hometown in South Carolina made Jackson's original Black Betsy and passed it to him through local trolley driver Captain Wesley Martin. Jackson had it trimmed and shaped by the Spalding Sporting Goods company at some point after his arrival in the big leagues. The bat, which was not originally dried or cured professionally had a telltale bend in it and, because Jackson later sent it to Spalding for a professional finishing, a Spalding insignia with the name of the company and the phrase Old Hickory.

Mike Nola, historian for the Joe Jackson's Virtual Hall of Fame website (www.blackbetsy.com), says the bat is legit. He relies on circumstantial evidence: It was one of the only bats Jackson owned when he died and had the famous bend in the wood that was often commented on and likely came from being made of unseasoned hickory; and the bat has a hairline crack suffered on a hit down the third-base line during a game in Waycross, Georgia, in 1924, after Jackson had been banished from professional ball.

But an article Nola cites about that game undercuts his argument. The local paper in Waycross has an article that bemoans the cracking, declaring that this bat was a personal favorite of Jackson, the one he had used throughout his major league career, even though Nola himself says Jackson rarely used the original Black Betsy in the majors for fear of breaking it and that he'd pull it out only in big games or if he was mired in a slump. There is also a letter cited in David Fleitz's biography, *Shoeless* from a Jackson cousin whose father managed a mill team in Greenville County in South Carolina after Jackson's banishment from the majors that says, "Joe often appeared at the team practices, demonstrating his swing for the eager mill hands with an ever-present replica of Black Betsy."

Further complicating the picture is the fact that the legend calls the original Black Betsy a behomoth, weighing 48 ounces, while the one sold and resold is 39.4 ounces.

Heritage Auctions had hyped its "evidence" by using an interview Jackson gave in the 1930s in which he said of the bat handed to him by Captain Martin, "I've had it ever since and it's never been broke, although it's getting old now and I expect it any time. I used to keep it soaked in a barrel of oil, but lately it's just been thrown by my desk in Savannah."

However, those are the recollections of an older man, one who also said, "I don't know just where the Cap'n got hold of it" even though years earlier he'd credited Charlie Ferguson with the job. The article on the Heritage Auction website also claimed that Jackson loaned Babe Ruth—then a pitcher with Boston—his prized possession, an unlikely occurrence that again makes this sound like the storytelling of an old ballplayer.

There were also stories in Greenville, North Carolina, that Jackson gave his original bat to the town's mayor. In *The Sporting News* in 1942, an article tells of how local children brought a gift for Jackson—a replica of the original Black Betsy. It then says, "The original bat reposes in the treasure chest of one of South Carolina's first families. It was given to the late Mayor John McHardy Mauldin of Greenvile when Shoeless Joe and baseball parted company."

Additionally, part of the lore says that in 1911 Jackson sent a duplicate of Black Betsy to Louisville Slugger to have copies made. That bat was lost in the company's factory fire in December 1910, and so Jackson was set to send them another back-up when he broke the original Black Betsy in spring training of 1911. Jackson then sent the broken bat to Louisville Slugger so they could base their copies on the original.

But that would mean the auctioned bat was not the original. Jackson named all his bats, but fans and reporters often called any bat he swung "Black Betsy." Further evidence supporting that argument comes from Fleitz's biography *Shoeless*. Fleitz found a Cleveland *Plain-Dealer* article from March 1911 that recounts how Jackson had indeed broken his bat during spring training. The article says the player was quite upset because he had "used no other [bat] the last three years." Given that the original Black Betsy was supposedly made in 1907 or 1908, that certainly sounds like the original bat that Jackson broke on that day.

And a recent reissue of F.C. Lane's book *Batting* throws another curve at the claim of authenticity of the auctioned Black Betsy. Lane was a sportswriter in the early 20th century and interviewed all the great hitters extensively. He quoted Jackson from an interview before his banishment from baseball in 1920. Jackson, explaining his loyalty to black bats, referred to the Captain

Martin bat by saying, "The bat he gave me was much the same as the one I use today and it was black. I have that original bat now although it is broken with hard usage. I would not take Five Hundred Dollars for it.... I have all my bats made after this one pattern and they are all black."

Collector Jim Johnson has a blog called White Betsy that makes several strong arguments against the Erwin bat: it is brown, not black, though Jackson was routinely photographed holding black bats during his career and never photographed with that particular bat; the bat is stamped Spalding Old Hickory Model 150, which was a retail model (but one that is different even from the Black Betsy retail models Spalding once sold). Johnson believes that Jackson may have switched to this lighter bat in his post-banishment, semipro days, a logical guess since he was 37 in 1924 when he was definitely using this bat.

The bat that people keep shelling out six figures for may be the original Black Betsy—it's impossible to say it ain't so for sure—but the evidence strongly implies that people are spending with their hearts and not their brains. However, they can at least be certain they are getting a bat that Jackson used and loved. He apparently taped the crack up after the Waycross incident and continued using it regularly afterward.

In 2004 another Jackson bat—made by Louisville Slugger around 1911 and featuring Jackson's signature—broke into the upper echelons when Hillerich & Bradsby sold it off for $137,000, edging out a Ty Cobb bat from the same auction that went for $132,000. H&B sold off those bats because they had others by those hitters and wanted money to fill in gaps in their collection. In fact earlier in 2004 the bat-maker had shelled out what was then the third-highest amount ever spent on a bat...although that is another story marked by controversy.

The bat Hillerich & Bradsby bought for $345,000 in the spring of 2004 was a bat used in 1941 by Joe DiMaggio during his 56-game hitting streak... supposedly. As soon as the bat been sold, however, the skeptics, who had been whispering beforehand, surfaced in public—particularly on Internet chat rooms—to claim that this was not a bat from the streak at all and even may not have been a bat DiMaggio ever used. Chief among the dissenters was Robert Plancich, an independent industry watchdog.

As with so many items in the baseball-memorabilia business there was no hard proof that this bat was the real deal. "There is always a wide time frame when the bat was used," Baseball Hall of Fame curator Ted Spencer said at the time. "With any bat, the credibility goes to the source."

The source initially seemed golden. The industry's top authenticator, Dave Bushing, rated the bat A10—which meant that the provenance of the bat was virtually guaranteed. However, Plancich countered that Bushing had undermined his credibility because he and the auction house, Mastronet, had not told H&B or other potential buyers that Bushing was not only the bat's authenticater…he was the one selling the bat. (Despite a top-flight reputation for helping to clean up the industry, Bushing has run into other problems like this, "authenticating" a Tom Seaver mitt as being from 1969—the Mets' World Series win would boost the value—when other experts easily identified that style of glove as not having been made until the mid-1970s; again Bushing was revealed as the seller.)

Photo Credit: Library of Congress, LC-DIG-ppmsca-18794

Joe DiMaggio loved the three bats that helped him create his 56-game hitting streak, but it's not certain that the one auctioned off in 2004 was one of them.

DiMaggio used only three bats during the streak. The first was stolen right before he set the record, so Tommy Henrich, who had been using one of DiMaggio's other bats gave him that bat back (after breaking the record with it, DiMaggio donated that Henrich bat for a USO auction). The original bat was then recovered, but in the last week of the streak Joe D. supposedly switched and brought out a new stick. This third bat was not heard from again for six decades. Then it supposedly resurfaced when Henrich's daughter Patricia Henrich discovered a DiMaggio Louisville Slugger in her grandmother's home.

Bushing decided it was a game-used DiMaggio bat from the early 1940s and paid Henrich $30,000, thinking he could re-sell it for more. Then Patricia Henrich called her father, who said it was from the streak and told her that DiMaggio had given it to him after it had cracked. For Bushing, that was good enough.

After the publicity of the $345,000 sale, however, problems quickly arose. DiMaggio had a track record of calling things what they weren't (he once "authenticated" a glove but got the decade completely wrong), and Henrich was a 91-year-old who, despite a healthy respect for the game's history, had apparently said nothing about this bat for all those decades. Could it be that the old man was conflating things or just thinking about the good ol' days?

"I don't want to disparage anyone here, but in this case, you have an old man who says he got the bat from Joe," Spencer said at the time. One New York *Daily News* story asserted that in independent interviews Henrich was "confused, or possibly evasive," and that his daughter then told the paper not to call him anymore.

One issue were the ball marks on the bat, which made it seem that the bat was used by a lefty (Henrich) as much as by a righty (DiMaggio), but Henrich said DiMaggio gave this third bat to him only after it cracked. Bushing hurt his cause further by arguing that photos show DiMaggio hitting with the label down, which would reverse the placement of the marks, but others quickly debunked this claim, along with other arguments that Bushing stretched to their breaking point.

Then Hillerich & Bradsby tried suing Plancich—dismissed by many in the memorabilia establishment as a crackpot—to shut him up, saying his campaign was derailing their plans to display the bat in their Louisville Slugger Museum. This further fueled the controversy within the industry, although a judge dismissed the case in 2005. (Much of this battle royale probably could have been averted had Bushing been forthright in his role; Bushing did give Patricia Henrich an undisclosed cut of the money and promised to disclose his financial arrangements in advance in the future.)

In the end, there are ways to counter every argument—the ball marks may be there simply because Henrich and DiMaggio often shared bats. As to why Henrich never did anything with the bat once he'd left it in his mother's

Photo Credit: Heritage Auctions

Finding bats from the 19th century that were used by the game's earliest stars is quite rare, so this Cap Anson bat brought home more than a quarter-million dollars.

house that year, maybe the letter the man known as Ol' Reliable wrote after the auction is true: "I got married, moved into my own home, and the war broke out, and that bat was soon forgotten. We really didn't pay much attention to this stuff back then."

Ultimately, some doubters were won over. Bat authenticator John Taube said he ultimately believed the bat was from the streak, although there's no way to prove it for sure. But Louisville Slugger spokesman Rick Redman says the company is completely satisfied that the bat is for real—former longtime employee Rex Bradley told them DiMaggio had mentioned giving the bat to Henrich—and so the company put the bat on display in their museum, declaring that it was one of three used during DiMaggio's great streak.

As difficult as it might be to certify a Ruth or DiMaggio bat, it gets even trickier the further back in time you travel. There are few authenticated game bats from the 19th century put up for sale and fewer still from baseball's handful of earliest heroes. So when Heritage Auctions put a genuine bat from Cap Anson up for sale in 2010, collectors swooned.

Cap Anson was 45 years old in 1897, finishing his career in Chicago, where he had played since the birth of the National League franchise in 1876. Anson was baseball's first superstar. He would finish with 3,435 hits and a .334 batting average. When he retired he was baseball's all-time leader in hits, runs scored, total bases, and RBI. (The first two marks lasted until Ty Cobb broke them a quarter-century later, while the last one survived until 1933 when Ruth finally caught Anson.)

The bat Anson used that season to collect his final hits was made by Hillerich & Bradsby sometime between 1894 and 1897, raising the possibility that Anson used the one bat for several years, possibly even to bang his 3,000th hit in 1894. The nail and three screws Anson drove into the barrel hint at the fact that he worked to repair this deep brown bat and keep it playable. (Ty Cobb used to do this too, claiming the rules against it were "a fool's law.") Anson clearly treasured the bat, carving 145 notches into the handle to improve his grip.

The bat remained in the Anson family until 2006 when it was sold off. That anonymous buyer then put it up for auction in 2010, along with a letter guaranteeing its authenticity from Anson's great-grandson. The hope was that it would reap $100,000, but Anson still had more pop in his bat, driving home a final bid of $286,000. That figure puts Anson in a formidable starting lineup alongside Ruth, Jackson, and DiMaggio as the men who swung the most valuable bats of all time.

FUNGOES, BATBOYS, DOUGHNUTS, METAL BATS
Some final accessories to good wood

> **Like it or not, the *crack* of the bat**
> **is inevitably being replaced by a *ping*.**
>
> *Hall of Fame commentator Peter Gammons,*
> *writing in* Sports Illustrated *in 1989*

The fungo bat is a baseball curiosity—most fans know the word fungo (even if only because it's such fun to say), yet few have seen one up close or ever used one.

Even at the pro level, where it is a vital part of everyday life, the fungo bat retains a bit of its mystery, as no one can pinpoint the origins of the bat… or the word. The practice of cutting a full-size bat in half to create a stick that was easier to self-hit fly balls seems to date to the 19th century; the word *fungo* was used as a verb in the Brooklyn *Daily Eagle* in 1892. Some speculate that the British term for playing cricket, "a fun go," is the basis for the word; others think it derives from the Scottish verb *fung* ("to toss or fling"), or the German verb *fangen* ("to catch"). Regardless, the fungo bat—longer, lighter, and skinnier than a regular bat—is a staple of the game.

The game's greatest fungo expert was Jimmie Reese, who is probably best remembered as Babe Ruth's roommate because of his quip, "I really roomed with the Babe's suitcase." But Reese, a Yankee in 1930 and 1931, was a baseball lifer, going from batboy to ballplayer to scout to minor league manager. Finally, in 1973, at age 71, Reese became a coach for the California Angels. He spent the last 22 years of his life in that role, developing friendships with Nolan Ryan (who gave a son the middle name Reese) and Reggie Jackson (who gave Reese the bat he used to tie Lou Gehrig on the career home run list) and cementing his stature as the King of the Fungo Hitters.

Reese won a bet with Chuck Tanner by hitting a flagpole with a batted ball 100 feet away on his first try, and he reportedly used only his fungo bat and a putter to shoot an 82 in 18 holes of golf. He would even "pitch" batting practice with his fungo bat, "throwing" strikes every time. (When the ball was thrown back to him, he'd pop up the ball with the bat so it landed in his free hand.) Reese could even fungo the ball right into the extended glove of a player lying on the grass 50 feet away.

Reese carved his own fungo bats—the store-bought variety didn't meet his standards—and even made one from the gift bat he received from Jackson. He loved his bats, which featured a wide, flat surface, and there are stories that circulate about the cruel fate a few of them met. According to one tale, an overweight minor league pitcher was so frustrated by Reese's fungo fielding drills in spring training that he shoved Reese's bat into the whirlpool, warping it. Another time, pitcher Chuck Finley accidentally broke the fungo made from Jackson's bat; horrified, Finley ran into the clubhouse and repaired it with finishing nails as best he could. When he died in 1994, Reese was buried in his Angels uniform, that same fungo bat resting by his side in the casket.

Today, even the fungo has been the muse for innovators—well-known science educator Bill Nye came up with an attachment for the end of the fungo that enables coach's to pick up a ball without bending down. "It's an older man's fungo," says Cade Griffis of D-Bats, which sells Nye's invention, called the "Skipper Stick." "It's a neat little novelty," he explains.

Batboys evolved from a novelty as well, though one of a very different nature. Before there were batboys there were mascots, such as Charles "Victory" Faust of John McGraw's New York Giants. Mascots, many of whom were physically handicapped, often were viewed as good-luck charms for superstitious ballplayers. Perhaps to legitimize their presence, mascots began taking on more responsibilities; by around 1910, their job title became "batboy."

Louis Van Zelst was a hunchback batboy who supposedly brought good luck to Connie Mack's Philadelphia A's while they won three World Series and four pennants from 1910-14. But the most famous batboy of all was the Yankees' Eddie Bennett. Born in Brooklyn, Bennett suffered a serious spinal injury as a child, then lost his parents in the 1918 influenza epidemic. The

Photo Credit: Library of Congress, LC-DIG-npcc-04915

Eddie Bennett, an orphan from Brooklyn, helped transform the role of batboy from being a good luck charm to a job with definite responsibilities.

following year, according to lore, Chicago White Sox outfielder Happy Felsch spotted the hunchbacked boy at the Polo Grounds (then the Yankees' home park) and, after he had a good game, briefly adopted Bennett as mascot/batboy. Little documentation exists regarding Bennett's role with Chicago, whose "Black Sox" threw the World Series that fall, but the next season Eddie wound up with Brooklyn. He apparently brought such good fortune that Brooklyn won the National League pennant and two of the first three games of the 1920 World Series. But when the National League champions left Bennett behind

when the Series moved to Cleveland, Brooklyn proceeded to drop four consecutive games and lost the best-of-nine Fall Classic. Some players claimed
Bennett's absence had jinxed them.

Bennett landed the batboy job with the Yankees in 1921—they won their
first pennant that season and seven during his 12 years there. Babe Ruth obviously deserves more credit than Bennett for that success, but Ruth was one of
Bennett's favorites, along with pitcher Urban Shocker (a Yankee from 1916-
17, 1925-28) and manager Miller Huggins. Bennett helped transform the image of his position—to the extent that Westbrook Pegler wrote he "raised the
job of batboy from a summer pastime to a solemn and responsible business"
by taking great care of bats and paying close attention to players' needs and
desires.

After getting hit by a taxicab in 1932, Bennett was forced to retire. Yankees owner Jacob Ruppert continued giving him money, but Bennett was lost
without baseball. He drank heavily and died in 1935. (The Yankees paid for
his funeral.)

In more recent times, Jay Mazzone was a prominent batboy for the Baltimore Orioles, serving from 1967-72 despite having lost both hands at age
2. Other batboys have gone on to celebrity in various fields. Novelist Thomas
Wolfe was a batboy in the minors in 1916; William Bendix, who grew up to
play the title character in the movie *The Babe Ruth Story*, had a brief stint as
Yankees batboy; Tiger Woods' father Earl served in the Negro leagues; Shirley
Povich got his baseball-loving son Maury a gig with the Washington Senators; Thad Mumford was a batboy before earning writing accolades, including
credits for 15 episodes of M*A*S*H (most notably in the much-acclaimed
finale of the hit television series); and sportscaster Roy Firestone was once on
the field handling the lumber as spring training batboy for the Orioles.

Another batboy, Charlie Grimm, achieved celebrity status in his own field,
moving on to a long career as a Cubs player and manager. Hall of Fame manager
Sparky Anderson once retrieved the timber under famed USC Trojans coach
Rod Dedeaux. Also, in the 1983 National League Championship Series, Los Angeles manager Tommy Lasorda gave the son of a good friend a turn as Dodgers
batboy for the games in Philadelphia—the lad's name was Mike Piazza.

Another bit of managerial patronage created the most memorable moment in batboy history. In Game 5 of the 2002 World Series, San Francisco's J.T. Snow raced home on a triple, only to find manager Dusty Baker's 3½-year-old son Darren prematurely dashing toward home plate to retrieve Kenny Lofton's bat. Snow scooped little Darren out of harm's way just before Giants baserunner David Bell followed Snow to the plate.

Fictional batboys have had their Hollywood-style moments in the sun. In addition to the bit parts played by batboys in *The Natural* and *Bull Durham*, the 1953 movie *The Kid from Left Field* virtually made a batboy the leading man. In this film, which starred Dan Dailey, Anne Bancroft, and Lloyd Bridges, a down-on-his-luck former ballplayer gets his son a job as a batboy, and the son gives the home-team manager and his players brilliant advice on how to improve their play. The team, not knowing that the genius behind the advice is really the father, makes the boy the manager as a publicity stunt. (The film was remade for television a quarter-century later and featured Gary Coleman and Robert Guillaume.)

Real life, as usual, often proves stranger and more intriguing than fiction. In the minor leagues, a batboy once even got into a game. In 1952, the Fitzgerald club in the Class D Georgia State League trailed 13-0 at Statesboro when fans started chanting, "Put in the batboy!" Astonishingly, Fitzgerald manager Charlie Ridgeway did just that. Joe Reliford, 12 years old and black, was sent up to pinch hit—he broke the league's color barrier in the process—and grounded sharply to third base. Later, he made a fine running catch to end an opposing player's 21-game hitting streak. Umpire Ed Kubrick, who approved Reliford's appearance, was fired the next day by the league, which also fined and suspended Ridgeway. (The penalties for Kubrick and Ridgeway in those segregated times may have had more to do with Reliford's race than his role as a batboy.)

Two other batboys earned more lasting fame, though one might be more properly called infamy. In 1969, California Angels third baseman Aurelio Rodriguez pulled a memorable prank when he switched uniforms with batboy Leonard Garcia and sent the youngster out for the photo session. The photographer didn't notice and one of Topps' most memorable "error" cards was born.

Boston Brave batboy Frank McNulty was also immortalized in the wrong uniform, but that was for artistic purposes. The great American artist Norman Rockwell needed a model for his classic illustration, "The Dugout," which features the hapless Chicago Cubs (some things never change) slumping helplessly on the bench while the opposing team's fans jeer and ridicule them.

Photo Credit: Library of Congress, LC-DIG-ppmsca-1847

Ty Cobb, seen here with Joe Jackson, was the first player to swing multiple bats in the on-deck circle.

But the picture is dominated by the forlorn batboy, who seems to be bearing the brunt of the hecklers. Rockwell was a New Englander and got McNulty, who later became president of *Parade Magazine,* to switch teams for art's sake. McNulty was paid only five dollars for his modeling work but he got a great bonus when Rockwell sent him a signed copy of the cover.

Just as John McGraw inadvertently helped pioneer the batboy job in his ceaseless quest for an edge over his opponents, another equally fiery combatant introduced another nuance to the game in his relentless pursuit of success.

In 1905 Ty Cobb was a rookie on the Detroit Tigers, looking to prove himself to his teammates and his opponents. Waiting in the on-deck circle, Cobb would swing three bats at once—it was something the savvy Cobb had done in the minor leagues because he'd realized that when he dropped two sticks en route to the plate his bat of choice felt far lighter. Many of Cobb's teammates looked at him with scorn, considering him a bit of a bush-league showoff. But nothing deterred Cobb. Not only did he eventually win most of them over with his hitting, he transformed what hitters did while waiting their turn.

The idea of using extra weight in the on-deck circle became a permanent part of the game. In the 1920s Heinie Groh swung a 54-ounce oak bat to prepare for his at-bats. By the 1930s some players had gone a step further and filled their extra bats with lead; a generation later, Elston Howard—the first black player to wear a Yankees uniform—introduced the idea of the dough-nut, a round 4-5 pound weight to slide over the player's game bat. By the early 1960s, he was hawking the Elston Howard On-Deck Bat Weight. (The "dough-nut" nickname came later.)

Recent scientific studies demonstrate that slowly swinging any weighted object in the on-deck circle actually slows a hitter's bat speed down. Batters would be better served by practicing their regular, short, quick swing with a single bat with no weights. Most professional players, however, choose to stick with the long-honored on-deck traditions instead of adjusting to what the research data shows.

There have been various gizmos and gadgets invented along the way, including Louisville Slugger's "whip-o-warm-up bat," which featured solid rubber and weighed five pounds but allowed for a whipping action; a Bratt on-deck bat that had a red plastic coating; and the 10-inch rubber-and-plastic weighted sleeves often seen today. Still, more than 100 years after Cobb swung three bats while awaiting his trip to the batter's box, most players prefer either multiple bats, the weighted bat, the sleeve, or the doughnut in the on-deck circle.

Inventors, however, never stop tinkering. And training devices for hitters have long popped up in the market—in the 1970s, there was "Power Swing," which had four plastic fins attached to a tube that created resistance during a swing and forced players to use a shorter, smoother stroke. The last decade has seen an explosion of products on the market—some are innovations and gimmicks and some are out there simply because there are so many new bat manufacturers. Numerous bat companies sell one-handed trainers or bats with heavy heads to strengthen the hands. The D-Bat Log, for instance, is 33 or 34 inches but weighs three ounces more. And many companies now offer bats that encourage a "whipping motion" to keep the bat inside the right zone, such as D-Bat's Underload Trainer, which remains skinny right up to its over-sized barrel. A company called Sklz markets numerous training bats, includ-ing the Sweet Spot Bat, which is a thin fiberglass rod with a wooden bat barrel attached to the end that helps batters feel the ideal contact spot and learn to whip the barrel into the hitting zone.

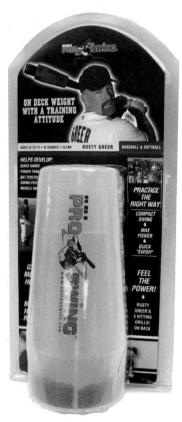

Photo Credit: RBI ProSwing

Hoping to improve his son's swing, Rick Miller invented the RBI ProSwing, designed to teach hitters the muscle memory for the proper contact point.

Then there are the bats like the Swing-Rite that click if you get the hands into the proper hitting area. But those are pricey, and in 2008 a Texan named Rick Miller decided to find a way to make an affordable variation when his son Brady was having trouble with the contact point of his swing. Miller created a sheath that slides over any bat; the RBI ProSwing, as he called it, has four chambers loaded with weights that make a swish sound at the moment of impact. "Click bats are all or nothing, but this gives you the sense of where you need to adjust," says Miller (who priced his invention at just $30). "It builds power and muscle memory at the same time."

More elaborate are tools like the WhipHit Bat and the Insider Bat that train a batter's hands to take the shortest path to the ball with an inside swing that prevents young hitters from casting out and around the ball. But neither of those are actual bats—the former relies on the rope and ball at the end of a pole to create proper technique, while the latter is metal with a flat swinging area to ensure the hitter meets the ball squarely.

A company called MetalWood Bats has its own variation that uses an actual bat...or two parts of one. About eight years ago, former major leaguer Jim Lefebvre approached the company with his idea—as a hitting instructor he had cut bats in half then put them back together with a makeshift hinge. The hinge technique "increases hand quickness and forces players to throw the bat head at the ball while revealing any flaws like rolling the wrists," company owner Jimmy

Tribble says. However, Lefebvre's homemade version "was like playing Russian Roulette—you'd never know when it would fly apart," says Jim Sovel, the company's vice-president of operations.

So the company designed the Hinge Bat, which separates the handle and barrel with a hinge welded into the aluminum handle and screwed into the wooden barrel; this patented design, Sovel says, not only works as a hitting tool—they say it increase a player's bat speed by 5-8 miles per hour—it was safe enough that they could get insurance coverage.

Obviously flying bat parts are a scary concept, but there's a more mundane pain that comes along with being a hitter. Whether you're a Little Leaguer playing on a cold April day or a major leaguer facing a 95-mile-an-hour cutter in on the hands, every batter striving to make hard contact knows he may get stung for his efforts. Batting gloves, which not only improve the grip but absorb the shock of bat-on-ball vibrations have become so ubiquitous that it's the players who don't wear them—Vlad Guerrero, Moises Alou, Jorge Posada, and a handful of others—that catch the eye these days. But batting gloves are a relatively modern phenomenon. (Of course, Alou is famous for claiming to urinate on his hands to toughen them, not a popular technique for most guys.)

Photo Credit: Jack Kasarjian

XProTeX gloves, pictured here, feature a rubber-esque composite on the glove to absorb the impact of a pitch on the hands, reducing the risk of injury.

Brooklyn's Lefty O'Doul reportedly wore a regular winter glove in 1932 to help soften the blow to an injured wrist. New York Giant Bobby Thomson and his teammate Johnny Mize in 1949 tried golf gloves in spring training and during cold weather batting practice. Ken Harrelson of Boston and later Kansas City is generally credited with being the first to wear a batting glove regularly during games in the 1960s. Like a golfer, Harrelson wore just one, on his bottom hand. Rusty Staub introduced the idea of wearing them on both hands to maximize the gripping potential, and by the 1980s the practice had become relatively common. These days, companies are bringing out ever more protective versions utilizing all sorts of technology that make the old style gloves look positively primitive. X Bat has moved to the head of the field with its new XProTeX gloves that feature a rubber-esque composite on the glove to absorb the impact of a pitch on the hands, reducing the risk of injury. (The company claims that a 100-mile-per-hour fastball would actually just have the impact of a 39-mile-per hour toss with the gloves on.) Batting gloves have led to all other kinds of armor for hitters to protect their wrists, elbows and shins.

Photo Credit: Easton

From the late 1970s through the 1990s, Easton dominated the metal bat market; in recent years the metal bat business has gotten considerably more crowded.

The single most important technological advance in the world of bats, of course, has been the advent of the metal bat. They are so dominant in baseball today that even a book on wood bats must devote a few words to their impact. The first patent for a metal bat is made in 1924 and a few were made in the 1930s, but at that point they were sturdy enough only for softball and too heavy to be practical. Technology improved over the decades, though, and aluminum bats finally came of age in the 1970s. The Worth Company introduced the first modern model in 1970, and soon Little League, high schools, and the NCAA approved metal bats.

Instantly popular because of their money-saving durability, metal bat sales took off, and by 1975 they'd surpassed wood. Easton passed Worth as the dominant metal bat-maker after it transformed the market with its 1978 bat the B5 Pro Big Barrel, which increased the barrel size and the bat's hitting power. Five years later they stepped up again in barrel size and technology. The company maintained its dominance until the 1990s.

Hillerich & Bradsby was slow getting into the game, and its early efforts were lackluster. It wasn't until the 1980s, when H&B hit a real slump in sales, that Jack Hillerich put serious energy and resources into the metal bat business. These days H&B makes its profit off metal bats, allowing the company to keep producing wood bats. Now, however, the competition is fierce, with Easton and H&B competing with Worth, Rawlings, and Wilson, among others. In 1993, a small company called DeMarini introduced a Doublewall bat to make the ball jump off even more quickly. (The company itself was snapped up by Wilson in 2000.)

But after a while, the technology of metal bats became too powerful, leading to games with football-like scores and the fear that pitchers and even infielders were in danger. This led to a series of regulations over the years designed to make aluminum bats play more and more like wood. The NCAA first created new rules in 1995 and tinkered with them repeatedly. In 2011, the BESR standard (Ball Exit Speed Ratio) was replaced with a new standard called BBCOR (Ball-Bat Coefficient of Restitution), which limits the amount of bounce at the moment of bat-on-ball contact. The result has been a decline in scoring but also a new challenge for bat-makers. "It's a tough thing," says Jim Darby, who has been with Easton since 1977. "We all try to make bats better than our competitors, but now can you say your bat will hit the ball further? No. The rules make them all the same. So it'll be about the grip and the cosmetics and other factors."

Another relatively new player in the amateur game is the composite bat. Major league hitters can only use bats made with one piece of wood, but for youth hitters looking for something that will last longer, companies have created an intriguing blend of materials.

Hillerich & Bradsby is producing composite wood bats utilizing aerospace-grade fibers, and some smaller companies are making a dent in the field with wood composite bats—especially with bamboo strips that can be pressed together to create a bat with the tensile strength of steel but the feel of a wood bat. Brett Brothers, owned by Hall of Famer George Brett and his brothers, features bats that are a mix of maple and bamboo, providing a durability far beyond anything that the single-piece bats allowed in pro ball can offer.

Another innovative newcomer to this field is the Radial Bat, created by a New Jersey entrepreneur named Ward Dill. The Radial features twelve wedges of wood joined together before being turned like a traditional bat on a lathe. The bat is touted as much more durable because more than one section of wood absorbs each contact with the ball; and even when it eventually might break there's little chance of it shattering like a modern maple bat. Additionally, the company is able to make them with drop weights up to -10, meaning a 30–inch bat could be as light as 20 ounces and thus much more manageable for Little Leaguers, encouraging them to switch from the ping of metal to the crack of wood.

Most intriguing of all is the modern-meets-traditional approach offered by the MetalWood Bat, created by Jimmy Tribble, a high school coach who wanted his players to hit with wood but couldn't afford the steady parade of broken bats. So he invented a perfect compromise: The MetalWood Bat has an aluminum handle to provide the durability that amateur programs from Little League to the NCAA rely upon, but it also has a wood barrel, which is safer for fielders and better training for batters. The company got approval from leagues in 2001, but launching the company and delivering the product has presented many obstacles, says Jim Sovel, vice-president of operations. "It's not easy getting a piece of aluminum to stay connected to a piece of wood when you have the force of impact from hitting a baseball," he points out. "And we didn't have our own engineering staff. We had to invent our own machines. It was all trial and error."

So, there are plenty of peripherals swirling around the story of the baseball bat, but at the center of it is still wood, good wood.

NAME INDEX

Aaron, Hank 13, 47, 87, 111
Abreu, Bobby 121
Adair, Robert 58
Agee, Tommy 7
Aiello, Danny 151
Ainsworth, Kurt 129
Allen, Dick 87
Allen, Mel 39
Alou, Felipe 46
Alou, Matty 47, 72
Alou, Moises 177
Altman, George 88
Anderson, Dave 52
Anderson, Jim 95, 97, 125
Anderson, Sparky 48, 172
Anson, Cap 28, 57, 110, 131, 167
Appel, Marty 47
Ashburn, Richie 28

Babe, Loren 42
Bagwell, Jeff 26, 91
Baker, Dusty 173
Baker, Frank 35, 111
Baker, Joe Don 146
Bancroft, Anne 173
Barnett, Larry 76
Beaumont, Linda 153
Bell, David 173
Belle, Albert 32, 61, 62
Beltran, Carlos 17, 129
Belushi, Jim 147
Bench, Johnny 33, 49, 101, 115, 155
Bendix, William 172
Beniquez, Juan 48
Bennett, Eddie 170

Bennett, John 101
Berra, Yogi 18, 21, 43, 135
Bichette, Dante 17, 31
Bickel, Fritz 113
Biggio, Craig 27
Black, Drew 65
Blomberg, Ron 46
Bochy, Bruce 81
Boggs, Wade 31, 32, 145
Bonds, Barry 46, 91, 95, 122, 141, 160
Boudreau, Lou 15
Bradley, Milton 10
Bradley, Rex 32, 167
Bradsby, Frank 111
Branca, Ralph 41, 42
Brauch, Steve 154
Braun, Ryan 123
Brett, George 67, 179
Bridges, Lloyd 173
Brinkman, Joe 68
Brown, Brown 112
Browning, Pete 107, 108
Brown, Willard 78
Buck, Jack 35
Buckner, Bill 58
Bumbry, Al 8
Burnett, A.J. 34
Bushing, Dave 165
Byrnes, Eric 94

Cabrera, Miguel 123, 124
Cain, Bob 25
Cammuso, Frank 141
Campanella, Roy 11, 78
Campaneris, Bert 76

Canseco, Jose 118, 145
Cant, Craig 128
Capone, Al 150
Carbo, Bernie 48
Cardenal, Jose 88
Carey, Andy 18
Carter, Gary 27, 58
Carter, Joe 53, 91, 122
Casey, Daniel 140
Cash, Norm 60, 63
Castilla, Vinny 17
Castillo, Luis 94
Castillo, Wellington 97
Castro, Ramon 94
Caudill, Bill 34
Cepeda, Orlando 32, 46, 87
Chance, Frank 110
Chandler, Happy 78
Chapman, Ben 78
Chihuly, Dale 155
Christopher, Matt 142
Chylak, Nestor 76
Clemens, Roger 75, 145
Clemente, Roberto 43, 87, 118
Coates, Jim 43
Cobb, Ty 8, 30, 51, 64, 71, 84, 85, 110,
        113, 164, 167, 174
Colbert, Stephen 76
Coleman, Gary 173
Collins, Eddie 28, 36, 111
Colvin, Tyler 97
Cooper, Cecil 63
Cooper, Stephanie 155
Cooper, Walker 118
Costner, Kevin 145
Crandall, Del 47
Crawford, Sam 37, 57, 59

Cronin, Joe 80
Cruise, Tom 146
Cruz, Jose 129
Curtis, Gavin 142

Dailey, Dan 173
Daley, Arthur 80
Darby, Jim 179
DaVanon, Jerry 68
Davis, Harry 111
Davis, Mike 52
Dawson, Andre 64
DeCinces, Doug 63
Dedeaux, ROd 172
Delgado, Carlos 122
DeLillo, Don 42
Dempsey, Jack 37
Dempsey, Rick 60
DeNiro, Robert 150
Dent, Bucky 50
Didier, Mel 53
Dill, Willard 180
DiMaggio, Joe 18, 38, 40, 42, 164
DiMuro, Lou 60
Doby, Larry 78
Douglas, Michael 147
Downing, Al 47
Doyle, Brian 50
Drew, J.D. 126
Drew, Stephen 126
Duffy, Hugh 17
Dunn, Adam 34, 99
Durham, Leon 28
Duvall, Robert 147
Duvall, Shelly 149
Dykstra, Lenny 63

Eastwick, Rawly 48
Eckersley, Dennis 52
Ellis, Dock 34
Erwin, Lester 161
Ewing, Buck 110

Fairly, Ron 74
Falzon, Jim 94
Faust, Charles 170
Feller, Bob 42
Felsch, Happy 171
Fennel, J. Paul 156
Ferguson, Bob 71
Ferguson, Charlie 30, 162, 163
Fielder, Cecil 17
Fine, Don 97, 100, 127
Finley, Chuck 170
Firestone, Roy 172
Fischer, Bill 43
Fisher, Jack 45
Fisk, Carlton 48
Fleitz, David 162
Floyd, Cliff 93
Ford, Dan 60
Foster, George 31
Fowler, Bill 40
Fox, Nellie 57
Frazier, George 69
Freehan, Bill 60
Freeman, Freddie 129
Fregosi, Jim 34
Frey, Jim 28
Frick, Ford 44
Frisch, Frankie 28
Fuentes, Tito 74
Fukudome, Kosuke 15

Gaedel, Eddie 24
Galbreath, John 44
Gallego, Mike 32
Gammons, Peter 169
Garcia, Leonard 173
Gehrig, Lou 37, 44, 119, 169
Gibson, Josh 78
Gibson, Kirk 35, 52, 118
Gibson, Mel 148
Giles, Warren 74
Gilligan, Lawrence and Joe 101, 124
Gioiosa, Tommy 64
Gonzalez, Adrian 126
Gonzalez, Luis 54
Goodman, Billy 23
Goslin, Goose 57, 68
Grace, Mark 27, 32
Granderson, Curtis 10
Grange, Red 37
Griffey, Ken, Jr. 89, 156
Griffis, Cade 100, 127, 170
Grimm, Charlie 172
Grimsley, Jason 61
Groat, Dick 43
Groh, Heinie 25, 174
Grove, Lefty 37
Guerrero, Vlad 126, 177
Guerrero, Wilton 61
Guidry, Ron 69
Guillaume, Robert 173
Guillen, Ozzie 62
Gunter, Archibald 140
Gutman, Dan 26
Gwynn, Tony 32, 89, 107

Haller, Tom 72
Harrelson, Ken 177

Harrelson, Woody 148
Harvey, Doug 58
Hatcher, Billy 60
Hatfield, John 72
Haysbert, Dennis 146
Hearst, William Randolph 139
Heath, Jeff 79
Heath, Mike 60
Heffernan, Gladys 80
Helling, Rick 93
Helms, Tommy 33
Helton, Todd 94
Hemus, Solly 23
Henderson, Rickey 127
Henrich, Patricia 166
Henrich, Tommy 22, 39, 165
Hensley, Clay 94
Hernandez, Roland 97
Herzog, Whitey 63
Heyward, Jason 129
Hicks, Hicks 72
Hill, Bob 107
Hillerich, J. Frederich 107, 109
Hillerich, John "Bud" 14, 107, 109, 111
Hillerich, John "Jack" A., III 114, 153,
    179
Hodges, Gil 11
Hodges, Russ 41
Holman, Sam 95, 117, 121
Hooten, Burt 49
Hopper, De Wolf 140
Hornsby, Rogers 86, 87
Hough, Charlie 49
Houk, Ralph 46
House, Tom 47
Howard, Elston 175
Huggins, Miller 172

Hunter, Torii 97

Incaviglia, Pete 10

Jackson, Bo 10
Jackson, Joe 28, 29, 131, 161
Jackson, Reggie 49, 118, 169
Janzen, Paul 51
Javier, Stan 96
Jeter, Derek 32, 54
Johnson, Andrew 152
Johnson, Ban 57, 59
Johnson, Darrell 48
Johnson, Davey 64
Johnson, Howard 28, 63
Johnson, Jim 164
Johnson, Lou 74
Johnson, Richard 125
Johnson, Willis 58
Jones, Charlotte 137
Jones, Chipper 16
Jones, James Earl 140

Kasarjian, Jack 124
Kay, Max 105
Keeler, Willie 22, 38, 110
Keillor, Garrison 141
Kelly, Mike 140
Kemp, Matt 118
Kendall, Jason 33
Kilmer, Joyce 133
Kiner, Ralph 118
King, Stephen 149
Kinst, Emile 101
Klein, Bonnie 156
Klesko, Ryan 121
Kluszewski, Ted 57

Koufax, Sandy 72
Kubek, Tony 43
Kubota, Isokazu 15, 16, 51, 119
Kubrick, Ed 173
Kuhn, Bowie 76
Kuklis, Kevin 127
Kuzmic, Craig 93

LaGrow, Lerrin 76
Lajoie, Nap 110
Lamberth, Chad 125
Lamont, Gene 61
Lane, F.C. 163
Lane, George 120
Lane, Kevin 95, 98, 119, 120, 124
Lane, Tom 120
Laplante, Michel 97, 100, 126
Larkin, Barry 18, 52, 129
Lasorda, Tommy 52, 172
Latham, Arnie 108
Lawrence, Joe 129
Lee, Spike 151
Lefebvre, Jim 176
Lemon, Bob 50
Lieberthal, Mike 124
Lofton, Kenny 173
Long, Dale 43
Long, Don 94
Lopes, Davey 47
Luckett, Danny 20, 113, 137

Mack, Connie 170
MacKenzie, Bill 121
MacPhail, Lee 68
Malamud, Bernard 143
Mantle, Mickey 18, 42, 44, 115
Marichal, Juan 72, 73

Maris, Roger 44
Marquard, Rube 35
Marshall, Willard 118
Martin, Billy 49, 67, 76
Martin, Captain Wesley 162
Martinez, Edgar 16, 17
Marucci, Jack 128
Mathewson, Christy 35
Matsui, Hideki 15, 16, 119
Mattingly, Don 18, 101, 102
Mauer, Joe 118
Mayberry, John 63
Mays, Willie 8, 13, 47, 74, 118
Mazeroski, Bill 43, 44, 53
Mazzone, Jay 172
McCarthy, Joe 38
McCatty, Steve 67
McClelland, Tim 62, 68
McClouth, Nate 94
McCovey, Willie 118
McDougald, Gil 18
McDowell, Roger 64
McGrath, Jack 35, 114
McGraw, John 25, 35, 110, 160, 170, 174
McGwire, Mark 46, 62, 160
McHardy, John 163
McKee, Jeff 100, 126
McKee, Steve 126
McLaughlin, Edwin 117
McNulty, Frank 173
McRae, Hal 63, 69
Meusel, Bob 38
Mifflin, Gary 157
Millard, Charles 117
Miller, Bob 74
Miller, Hack 22
Miller, Rick 176

Mize, Johnny 17, 19, 118, 177
Mizuno, Rihacki 15, 119
Morales, Jose 28
Morgan, Joe 23
Morris, Hal 61
Morrow, Henry 113
Mosquera, Julio 93
Moyer, Jon 125
Mumford, Thad 172
Munson, Thurman 49
Murphy, Dale 18, 28
Musial, Stan 23, 24, 27, 43, 86

Napoli-Tejada, Marcia 160
Nettles, Graig 60
Newcombe, Don 78
Nicholson, Jack 149
Nielsen, Leslie 149
Nola, Mike 30, 162
Nunn, Bill 151
Nye, Bill 170

Oberkfell, Ken 18
Ochiai, Hiromitsu 16
Odom, John 81
O'Doul, Lefty 177
Oldenburg, Charles 153
Olivo, Miguel 94
O'Neill, Paul 91
O'Nora, Brian 95
Orsatti, Victor 160
Orsulak, Joe 32
Ortiz, David 55, 99
Otis, Amos 63
Otsuka, Akinori 81

Pafko, Andy 41

Patterson, Red 42
Pegler, Westbrook 172
Pena, Alejandro 52
Pena, Tony 64
Pennington, Cliff 95
Perez, Eduardo 129
Perez, Tony 8
Perry, Gaylord 63
Pesci, Joe 148
Phillips, Dave 61
Phoenix, Joaquin 148
Piazza, Mike 172
Pickett, Jack 110
Piniella, Lou 63
Pinson, Vada 57
Pitt, Brad 150
Plancich, Robert 164
Podsednik, Scott 27
Posada, Jorge 177
Povich, Maury 172
Presley, Elvis 10
Pujols, Albert 89, 129
Pusser, Buford 146

Quantrill, Paul 55
Quick, Jim 67

Ramirez, Manny 124
Randolph, Willie 50
Reach, A.J. 110
Redford, Robert 143
Redman, Rick 167
Reese, Jimmie 169
Reliford, Joe 173
Reyes, Jose 129
Reynolds, Burt 148
Rhodes, Susan 95

Rickey, Branch 78
Ridgeway, Charlie 173
Ripken, Cal, Jr. 115
Ritter, Lawrence 25
Rivera, Mariano 54, 91, 130
Rivers, Mickey 50
Rizzuto, Phil 141
Robinson, Jackie 11, 77, 79, 131, 142
Rockwell, Norman 174
Rodriguez, Alex 20
Rodriguez, Aurelio 173
Rogers, Jack 156
Rogers, Kenny 147
Roseboro, Johnny 72, 73
Rose, Pete 8, 23, 31, 51, 64, 66, 83, 119
Roth, Eli 150
Roush, Edd 21, 23
Runge, Paul 64
Ruppert, Jacob 172
Russell, Bill 47, 96
Russell, Kurt 148
Ruth, Babe 7, 9, 20, 21, 37, 44, 47, 49,
        57, 59, 65, 84, 87, 113, 115, 126,
        159, 169, 172
Ryan, Nolan 169

Saar, Alison 152
Sabo, Chris 61
Salmon, Tim 96
Sanguillen, Manny 32
Saucier, Frank 25
Sauer, Hank 83
Schmidt, Mike 50, 118
Schubert, Bill 65
Schulz, Charles 141
Schumacher, Hal 41, 117
Schupp, Chuck 18, 27, 91, 137

Schuster, Michael 154
Scott, George 8
Seaver, Tom 165
Seely, Hart 141
Segui, David 125
Selmeier, Joel 155
Severeid, Hank 21
Sewell, Joe 10
Sfirri, Mark 156
Shaw, Skip 103
Shocker, Urban 172
Shyamlan, M. Night 148
Simmons, Al 22
Simpson, Homer J. 144
Sisler, George 38, 57, 113
Skowron, Moose 43
Smith, Dave 60
Smith, Hal 43
Smith, Ozzie 145
Smith, William 156
Snider, Duke 11
Snow, J.T. 173
Sorrento, Paul 61
Sosa, Elias 49
Sosa, Sammy 46, 62, 124
Sovel, Jim 177, 180
Spalding, Albert G. 84, 110
Speaker, Tris 21
Spencer, Jim 50
Spencer, Ted 165
Sprague, Ed 122
Stallar, Tracy 45
Stanky, Eddie 78
Stanton, Frank 155
Stargell, Willie 32, 83
Staub, Rusty 178
Stearnes, Turkey 18

Steinbach, Terry 34
Steinbrenner, George 69
Stengel, Casey 43
Stirt, Alan 157
Stobbs, Chuck 42
Strawberry, Darryl 145
Suttles, Mule 22
Suzuki, Ichiro 15, 119
Swan, Craig 31

Tanner, Chuck 170
Tarantino, Quentin 150
Taube, John 66, 167
Taubensee, Ed 61
Terry, Bill 40
Terry, Ralph 44
Thayer, Ernest Lawrence 139
Thompson, Henry 78
Thomson, Bobby 41, 117, 177
Tilden, Bill 37
Torgeson, Earl 32
Torre, Joe 118
Torrez, Mike 50
Tribble, Jimmy 177, 180
Trudeau, Charles 124, 130
Trudeau, Rusty 104
Tulowitzki, Troy 118, 123
Turturro, John 151

Utley, Chase 130

Van Zelst, Louis 170
Vaughan, Porter 40
Veeck, Bill 24, 78
Vesery, Jacques 156
Virdon, Bill 43

Waggoner, Carus 153
Wagner, Honus 28, 84, 110, 111, 160
Walker, Harry 30, 31
Weaver, Earl 58
Weissman, Andy 100
Wells, Jim 93, 95, 100, 102
Weyhing, Gus 108
White, Roy 7, 50
Williams, Ken 57
Williams, Mitch 53
Williams, Ted 7, 13, 14, 40, 44, 80, 83,
    86, 104, 113
Wills, Maury 72
Wilson, August 151
Wilson, Hack 26
Wilson, Roger 33
Wise, Rick 48
Wolfe, Thomas 172
Wolinsky, Mrs. Peter 79
Wolter, Steve 52, 65
Woods, Earl 172
Woods, Tiger 172
Wright, David 129
Wright, George 110

Yastrzemski, Carl 20
Yeager, Steve 95
Yvars, Sal 32

Zachary, Tom 38
Zambrano, Carlos 10

Other Books from ACTA Sports

SOLID FOOLS' GOLD
Detours on the Way
to Conventional Wisdom
Bill James
The founder of sabermetrics is back with witty, insightful, and just plain fun articles on everything from the best starting rotations and the worst teams of all times to the predictability of RBI and how the "Expansion Time Bomb" will affect future Hall of Fame selections. 207-page paperback, $14.95

TRADED
Inside the Most Lopsided Trades
in Baseball History
Doug Decatur
Uses Bill James' Win Shares to analyze some of the most infamous trades in history and identifies thirteen red flags that might indicate a lopsided trade when it occurs today. (189-page paperback, $19.95)

STRAT-O-MATIC FANATICS
The Unlikely Success Story of a Game
That Became an American Passion
Glenn Guzzo
The true story behind the creation—and re-creation—of America's most popular sports board game ever. Tells the story of Hal Richmond, founder of Strat-O-Matic, who beat the odds and built a company that continues to thrive in a highly competitive industry. 317-page paperback, $14.95

THE LIFE OF LOU GEHRIG
Told by a Fan
Sara Kaden Brunsvold
Highlights the human stories from Gehrig's life that fill in the gaps between the facts, such as his cures for hitting slumps, his favorite foods, and even his woeful attempt at comedy with Babe Ruth. 252-page paperback, $14.95

WALK OFFS, LAST LICKS,
AND FINAL OUTS
Baseball's Grand
(and not-so-grand) Finales
Bill Chuck and Jim Kaplan,
Foreword by Jon Miller
The definitive collection of baseball's final acts, including the greatest postseason finishes, every perfect game, last moments of distinguished old stadiums, greatest games ever played, and enough random facts and figures to satisfy the most devoted trivia addict. 213-page paperback, $14.95

THE NEW BALLGAME
Understanding Baseball Statistics
for the Casual Fan
Glen Guzzo, Foreword by John Dewan
Provides a user-friendly explanation of sabermetrics, the increasingly complex statistics used in the game of baseball, the subject of the popular movie *Moneyball*. 167-page paperback, $14.95

Available from Booksellers or Call 800-397-2282
www.actasports.com